PEOPLE WHO INFLUENCED THE
WORLD
OVER THE PAST 100 YEARS

PEOPLE WHO INFLUENCED THE
WORLD
OVER THE PAST 100 YEARS

Compiled by
PETER MURRAY

with international commentator
RAJGOPAL NIDAMBOOR
Contributing editor
SREERAM CHAULIA

Murray Books

First published in 2005 by
Murray Books (Australia)
www.murraybooks.com

ISBN 0-9580348-5-0

1. Celebrities - Biography. 2. History,
Modern - 20th century 920.2

Design and Production: Peter Murray
Editor: Victoria Shepherd

My thanks to Raj – my brother in India for his invaluable help and assistance in the making of this book.
Thanks also to Sreeram Chaulia who provided a valuable insight into some of the subjects.
Thanks also to The White House, Washington DC. and Wikipedia Encyclopedia.

Images: Headpress Australia

C O N T E N T S

INTRODUCTION

This has been a rewarding task and one that was difficult in the initial selection phrase. There have been many who influenced the world over the past one hundred years including scientists, thinkers, dictators and tyrants, heros and icons, builders and titans, artists and entertainers, leaders and revolutionaries and spiritual leaders.

From our recent past we have included inspirational leaders like Nelson Mandela who, with F.W. de Klerk, changed the face of South Africa forever. Mikhail Gorbachev engineered the shut down of the Soviet Empire and during the administration of Bill Clinton, the U.S. enjoyed more peace and economic well being than at any time in its history. We have also featured inspirational leaders from our past including Margaret Thatcher, Sir Winston Churchill and Jawaharlal Nehru.

Numerous artists and entertainers have developed our way of life and culture including Elvis Presley, Marilyn Monroe, Charlie Chaplin, Frank Sinatra and Pablo Picasso who was at the very top of the creative genius pyramid. The Beatles changed the way we listen to music during the 60s and early 70s. They were the most influential and successful popular music group of the rock era.

Where would the world be without the heros and icons of the past century? John F. Kennedy was the youngest and most popular American President, he was the singular source of hope for the baby boomer generation. Princess Diana was a fashion icon, an ideal of feminine beauty, admired and emulated for her high-profile involvement in AIDS issues and the international campaign against landmines.
Aung San Suu Kyi, is an outstanding woman who epitomised the eternal human pursuit of democracy, dignity and decency in her fight for a free Burma. Mother Teresa is assured of her dignified place in human history - a true saint in her own lifetime. Helen Keller was the internationally celebrated disabled rights activist and feminist who conquered crippling physical handicaps with indomitable willpower. Coco Chanel was an icon in the fashion industry – she was passionate about clothing design and a trendsetter whose influence can still be seen today.

Of the great scientists and thinkers, we have included David Suzuki who popularised science in Canada and other parts of the world with untiring energy for more than three decades. Jacques Cousteau is admired worldwide through the many who love the sea, and is still regarded highly for his devotion to adventure, nature and exploration. Henry Ford was an entrepreneur beyond compare, and besides his love for cars, he had several other interests - he was a master of finance, he knew the potential of plastics. He used them in Ford automobiles throughout the 1930s. He also patented a light-weight automobile, made entirely of plastic. It ran on grain alcohol, or ethanol alcohol fuel, instead of gasoline.
He was ahead of his time.

Of our featured dictators and tyrants, Osama bin Laden was the man who single-handedly polarised public opinion with horrifying acts of violence, prompting scholars to brand him the causative for 'World War III'. An arch terrorist mastermind to some and a heroic freedom fighter to others, he rejuvenated Islamic extremism to take on the mightiest of powers. His life vindicated the truism that charismatic individuals influenced the course of history.

Enjoy this walk through history.

Peter Murray

CONTENTS

Aung San Suu Kyi

1945 –

Burma's Heroine

Aung San Suu Kyi, is an outstanding woman who epitomised the eternal human pursuit of democracy, dignity and decency. In the words of former Czech President Vaclav Havel, she was a silver lining not only for the Burmese people trampled by military dictatorship, but also 'For all those who want to be free to choose their own destiny.'

An uncompromising force for self–determination, she set high standards in civil courage and non–violence that aroused international public opinion and induced governments to reassess the importance of human rights in their foreign policies.

Suu Kyi was born in Burma's capital Rangoon, theatre of a political maelstrom that decisively tuned her character. Her father Aung San was a national hero who led the fight for freedom against the British with the help of the Japanese. However, he saw through the dangers of Japanese occupation and worked for real independence for the Burmese from all types of imperialism. Right-wing opponents assassinated him when Suu Kyi was just two years old. Burma had a false dawn at independence in 1948, with no civilian leader of stature to steer. As the country tottered towards militarism, Suu Kyi never forgot that she was her father's daughter, destined to restore

Burma to people's sovereignty. She was steeled by her father's loyalists to believe so.

From earliest childhood, Suu Kyi was preoccupied with what she could do to help fellow Burmese. Although a resident of distant lands, she remained attuned to Burmese politics. Her mother brought her up in Burmese social values and Buddhism. In spite of long stints abroad, Suu Kyi's endearing Burmese mannerisms were intact thanks to a traditional upbringing. In 1961, her mother was appointed ambassador to India. Suu Kyi continued her education in New Delhi, hobnobbing with elites and enjoying diplomatic privileges. Reading was her major hobby. The teachings and practices of Mahatma Gandhi especially captivated her.

In 1964, Suu Kyi entered Oxford University to study Politics, Philosophy and Economics. She justified the choice to an interviewer: 'I did it because Economics seemed to be of most use for a developing country'. An intellectually inquisitive girl, she was engrossed by a trip to Algeria, which was slowly recovering from French despotism. In 1967, Suu Kyi went to New York and worked as a research assistant at the United Nations Advisory Committee on Finance, devoting weekends to voluntary work at the Belleview hospital that cared for New York's

▶ Burma's Heroine

Previous page: Aung San Suu Kyi, is an outstanding woman who epitomised the eternal human pursuit of democracy, dignity and decency.
Opposite: The more she sacrificed the greater the love and adulation she received from her supporters.

derelict. An attempt to interrogate and trouble her by representatives of the Burmese military failed when she resolutely defended her legal status in the U.S.

Marriage to a British scholar carried Suu Kyi to Bhutan and then back to Oxford in the seventies. Homemaking and motherhood did not stunt her intellectual bent of mind. The essential Aung San Suu Kyi was sculpted in those difficult days. She published a biographical essay on her father in 1984 and followed it with other insightful writings on Burmese thought, culture and history.

In 1987, Suu Kyi enrolled for a Ph.D in Burmese literature at London University. However, fate intervened irrevocably when her mother fell seriously ill in Burma the following year. Suu Kyi arrived in Rangoon as a full–blown anti–military junta uprising was getting off the ground. Trigger–happy soldiers mercilessly mowed down thousands of unarmed students, doctors, nurses and monks across Burma's landscape. After self–introspection, Aung San's heir decided, 'This is not a time when anyone who cares can stay out.'

Suu Kyi's political debut left no doubt that she was a focussed tactician who craftily combined the cry for human rights with 'Burma's second struggle for independence.' Though antagonistic to military rule, she confessed 'Strong attachment' to the armed forces that defended Burma from foreign aggressors. Her point was that the army as an institution must be respected, provided it submitted to the people's will. 'Be loyal to the people', was her trademark slogan addressed to the army. Reconciliation between military and civilian leaders appeared to be the only hope of saving Burma from more bloodshed. Non–confrontational by nature, she always sought ways out of impasses. In 1988, Suu Kyi formed the National League for Democracy (NLD) in defiance of a

new ban on political activity, amidst worsening state atrocities against citizens. She fearlessly toured the length and breadth of the country, kindling a mass craving for freedom. Her whirlwind trips and magnetism drew western media comparisons with Gandhi's civil disobedience movement. The Rangoon government arrested her followers and spread wild rumours about her personal life as a 'foreign woman' in a bid to cap the erupting volcano. Government harassment reached a pinnacle when an officer ordered Suu Kyi to be shot in April 1989. She walked up to the firing squad of six soldiers and disarmed it with moral power.

In July 1989, Suu Kyi was put under house arrest, the first of many punitive internments. On several occasions, the junta offered to set her free if she left for exile, but she firmly fended off compromise. Burma was her motherland and she had made up her mind to stay there as a powerful symbol that kept the struggle alive at home and drew international condemnation overseas. She was prevented from campaigning for or contesting the 1990 elections, which the junta tried to manipulate. Yet, NLD swept the polls. Though people voted for Suu Kyi's party, a vicious crackdown on NLD ensued. Ignoring her federalist remedy to the problem of ethnic minorities, the junta prosecuted bloody wars against Karen, Karenni and Kachin rebels and plunged Burma into an abyss.

Crowned with the Nobel Peace Prize in 1991, Suu Kyi's collection of awards received in absentia grew in size even as the junta held her in continuous captivity with brief interludes. The more she sacrificed (failing to attend even her husband's funeral), the greater the love and adulation she received. Notwithstanding Suu Kyi's unfinished mission as of 2005, the votive flame she lit was already assured an immortal place in world history.

John F. Kennedy

1917 – 1963

The most popular U.S. President

John Fitzgerald Kennedy was a political mete-or that shimmered briefly on the American skyline but left everlasting memories and longings. The youngest and most popular American President, he was the singular source of hope for the baby boomer generation. A magnetic personality that promised so much to so many, he enjoyed unparalleled fame and repute across the world while alive and left extreme sorrow and disbelief in the wake of his mysterious assassination. In the words of historian Arthur Schlesinger, 'He glittered when he lived, and the whole world grieved when he died.'

Kennedy was born with the proverbial silver spoon to Boston–based Irish Catholic parents hailing from prominent political and business lineages. His philandering millionaire father was involved in banking, Hollywood, stock markets and national–level politics. Kennedy, pet–named 'Jack', suffered many bouts of ill health in childhood and was psychologically scarred by a dysfunctional family. He was constantly quizzed by his ambitious father on current events and developed a love for history as a subject at an exclusive private boarding school.

As a teenager, Kennedy found doors to prestigious universities in Britain and in the U.S. opening because of his father's influence. The achievements of the young Kennedy were largely a case of greatness being thrust upon a mediocre scion. His professor at Harvard labelled him 'Gregarious, irreverent, far from diligent.'

As Europe hurtled toward World War II, Kennedy developed a special interest in foreign affairs. His father's shrewdness ensured that his bachelor's thesis on British appeasement of Hitler was polished and engineered into a bestseller entitled 'Why England Slept.' Aged 23, Kennedy had become a young superstar in America, living up to his father's dictum that 'A book that really makes the grade with high–class people stands you in good stead for years to come.'

Kennedy's frail health was a hurdle to qualifying for the peacetime draft in 1941, but mindful of the value of wartime record for a future career in politics, his father stage–managed his admission into the U.S. navy. By 1943, Kennedy was made skipper of a patrol boat in the Solomon Islands which was torpedoed by a Japanese destroyer. He showed exemplary bravery and rescued crewmen. The Kennedy public relations machine turned the heroism into legend and constructed a mythology by exaggeration.

Kennedy's elder brother's plane crash drove him inexorably to a career in American politics after the war. He ran for the U.S. House of Representatives from Boston on

▶ The most popular U.S. President

Previous page: A magnetic personality that promised so much to so many, Kennedy enjoyed unparalleled fame and repute across the world while alive and left extreme sorrow and disbelief in the wake of his mysterious assassination. Opposite: Kennedy inspects the Apollo landing module. In his September 12, 1962 speech at Rice University, he announced his new space programme.

the Democratic ticket, appealing directly to the voters' needs and aspirations. His callow charm offensive, coupled with the family fortune, guaranteed victory in 1946. Once in the House in Washington, Kennedy had an unremarkable start. One friend commented, 'Jack had been a fish out of water' who initiated no original legislation. Like most compatriots, he was a rabid anti–Communist who appreciated McCarthyist purges, approved greater defence spending and believed in the Truman Doctrine's dominoes theory. Kennedy was a product of the Cold War.

Goaded by soaring ambition, he ran for the Massachusetts Senate in 1952, defeating veteran politicians and winning Protestant votes. His father's golden rule came in handy: 'It takes three things to win in politics. The first is money, the second is money, and the third is money.'

Kennedy as a Senator was relatively undistinguished. He married Jacqueline Bouvier to overcome the politically hurtful tag of playboy and expressed an interest in the Presidency as early as 1954. In 1956, he allegedly ghost wrote 'Profiles in Courage', which was awarded the Pulitzer Prize. This book rocketed his reputation onto the world stage. After losing a bid to the Vice Presidential Democratic nomination in the same year, he strategically planned a rising profile through speeches, articles and the social circuit. Kennedy was at home in the realms of glitz and pizzazz.

In 1960, Kennedy trounced Hubert Humphrey for the Democratic Presidential nomination, carrying Catholic and Protestant votes. Former President Harry Truman remarked about the role of Kennedy's father in this victory: 'Joe paid for everything.' Kennedy defeated Republican Richard Nixon narrowly in the November election, capitalising on televised debates and his hand-

some image of youthful vitality that suggested the dawning of a new era.

President Kennedy had a mixed record. He continued Eisenhower's disastrous policy of training insurgents to overthrow Fidel Castro in Cuba and ended up with egg on his face with the Bay of Pigs fiasco. His hardliner attitude against the U.S.S.R. deepened U.S. military involvement in the greatest American foreign policy Waterloo, Vietnam. The maturity and prescience with which he handled the Cuban missile crisis earned him the status of statesman, although some criticised his reckless bravado.

On the domestic front, Kennedy and his brother, Attorney General Robert, championed the evolving civil rights movement. They invoked federal powers and got racially discriminatory mechanisms dismantled. One big vested interest that they ran into was the FBI, which resisted the entry of black officers. Kennedy tried guiding the racial equality agitation into softer channels, aware of the need to prevent polarisation of society and his own vote banks. He advanced liberalism by placing faith in governmental action to rectify social iniquities via the 'New Frontier' welfare package.

In 1963, as Kennedy deliberated on 'How to get out of Vietnam', he was shot dead in Dallas. It was a supremely tragic event in American history, one that left harrowing questions for decades. Americans were scandalously cheated by the unsolved mystery of the conspiracy behind the killing. Such was the shock of Kennedy's passage that they never forgot what they were doing on that fateful day when 'JFK' was felled. Posthumously, he was immortalised in books, films and the media, fulfilling the deep American sense of nostalgia for the Camelot vision he had conjured.

Anne Frank

1929 - 1944

Destiny's child

Anne Frank was destiny's child who attained dizzying heights at an incredibly young age. Her potential as a sensitive diarist, poet and social commentator never bloomed fully owing to the cruelty of circumstances. Yet, whatever she wrote in a truncated life of 15 years was translated into more than 60 languages, adapted to theatre, film and television. A muse who thought far ahead of her tender teenage years, her courage and grace under distress moved millions and brought home the import of fortitude under persecution. This gritty little girl cracked the puzzle of how humans cope with fear, more convincingly than any expert psychologist.

Frank was born in Frankfurt, Germany, to a respected Jewish businessman, one of the entrepreneurs who turned the city into a financial citadel of the western world. Affectionate parents, nurses and relatives doted on her in a spacious flat during a comfortable early childhood. In the summer of 1933, Frank's father decided to pre-empt Hitler's advancing shadow of anti-Semitism and took refuge in Holland, where he re-established trade in a food products company. Four-year-old Frank fled with her mother and sister to Aachen on the Belgian border, scarcely understanding the import of the tumultuous events that were shaping her destiny. After a few months at her grandmother's place, she reunited with her father in Amsterdam. In the backdrop of the rising storm of Nazism, Frank led the life of an average Dutch girl for the rest of the 1930s. 'I have darling parents, relations who are darlings too and a good home. I don't seem to lack anything', she reflected. She went to the Montessori School, boasted 'About thirty people whom one might call friends' and developed tastes for boyfriends and other mundane delights of life.

In 1940, Hitler invaded Holland, forcing the Dutch royalty to escape to England. Struggling with the looming identity of a Jew who had to prominently display the yellow star, Frank mourned the deposed Dutch monarchs who had offered asylum to the maltreated. 'It surprises the others that I should be so keen on the royal family'.

As Nazi tyranny took effect, Frank had to quit the common school and join the Jewish Lyceum in 1941. Her farewell to a favourite teacher at Montessori was very tearful: 'I had to say goodbye to Mrs. K. We both wept, it was very sad.' Frank's prescient father began arranging a safe place for the family after he was forced to formally quit business by anti-Jewish decrees. In 1942, Hitler's executioners sent a 'Call-up notice' to Frank's older sister.

▶Destiny's child

Previous page: Anne Frank witnessed the swings of war in Holland through the curtain slits of the annex and recounted them meticulously in the diary. Opposite: Frank's ordeal was sweetened by insights into beauty, creativity and love, peppered with a cheeky sense of humour.

I was more frightened than ever – Margot is sixteen. Would they really take girls of that age away alone?' she asked aloud. The very next day, the Franks clandestinely shifted to the hiding spot in an office building of Amsterdam.

Terrified by the roundup–cum–deportations of Jews and apprehensive of being discovered in their 'Secret Annex', the Franks survived a hushed life with another Jewish family for the next two years. Seven mortified individuals shared scanty space in a prison of sorts. Some of the darkest forebodings of Frank's mind needed an outlet. She jotted thoughts into a diary that was irregularly entered due to the stress of fast–paced political changes. She was also aware that a quotidian diary with run–of–the–mill facts would be boring for her imaginary friend, 'Kitty'. She only wrote when there was something worthwhile to be communicated. Frank was a highly perceptive adolescent who needed someone to confide in. 'Kitty', her creation, would be the privileged recipient of those innermost sentiments.

Less than a week into concealment, 'Kitty' heard from the stifled soul: 'I can't tell you how oppressive it is never to be able to go outdoors. Also, I'm very afraid that we shall be discovered and be shot.' Frank adjusted smilingly to hunger better than a mature adult. She made the most of what she had and appraised a jumper knitted out of coarse wool with cool practicality: 'As long as its warm, that's all that matters.' She elaborated on the pangs of growing up and adjusting to social and gender mores. Her impatience against petty human nature found expression in the claustrophobic milieu.

Frank read voraciously in the annex, besides listening to radio broadcasts from London, New York and Tel Aviv about the war's fortunes. Journalism, as a profession, attracted her. The travails totally fortified her moral fibre. 'I believe that God wants to try me. I must become good through my own efforts.' While admitting an eighth stowaway into the annex in November 1942, she cited her magnanimous father: 'If we can save someone, then everything else is of secondary importance.' Her powers of observation were acute. She witnessed the swings of war in Holland through the curtain slits of the annex and recounted them meticulously in the diary.

An abiding theme of Frank's diary was hope for the return of good times. She imagined life after the war was over. 'The time will come when we are people again, and not just Jews.' Ensconced in the relatively secure annex, she felt guilty for the locals caught up in the Nazi vortex and Dutch collaborators who risked everything to help Jews.

Frank's ordeal was sweetened by insights into beauty, creativity and love, peppered with a cheeky sense of humour. Her lesser–known writings included stories, fairytales, essays and reminiscences. They glowed with sympathy for the plight of girl children and the poor. Frank discerned the folly behind manufacturing fighter airplanes and bombs. In her unfinished novel, 'Cady's Life', she established the inseparability of freedom and justice and identified the elusiveness of world peace.

In August 1944, the Nazi secret police busted Frank's redoubt. She was transported to Auschwitz and thence to Belsen concentration camp in Germany, where she died waiting for the liberating Allies. Anne Frank wanted to go on living even after her death. The world recognised her posthumously as a voice of conscience and vowed to never again allow genocide to happen, an insincerely kept promise that failed to honour her legacy.

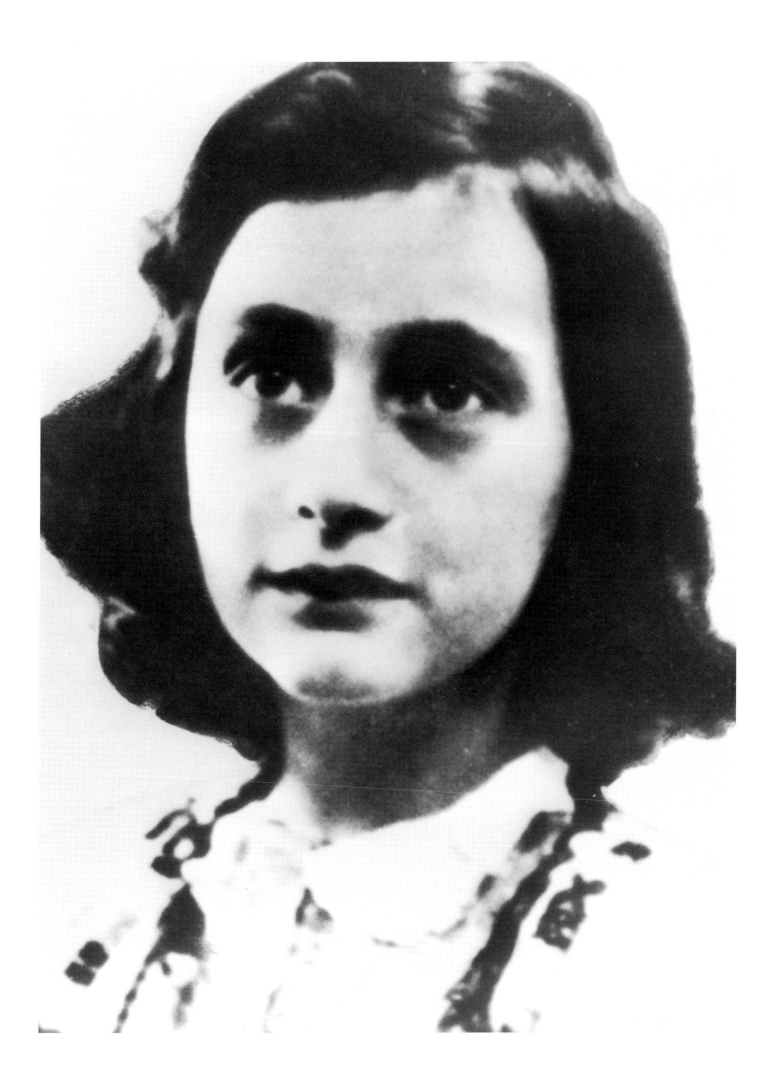

Helen Keller

1880 – 1968

Disabled rights activist

Helen Adams Keller was the internationally celebrated disabled rights activist and feminist who conquered crippling physical handicaps with indomitable willpower. Acclaimed as one of America's most noteworthy women leaders, she burrowed her way out of darkness through pluck and a never–say–die attitude. Where ordinary ill–fated mortals would have resigned themselves to a listless existence on the margins of society, she waged a hard–won battle for a significant life. Mental toughness was her greatest bequest.

Keller was born a normal healthy child in Alabama, southern U.S.A., to a wealthy civil war veteran who edited a weekly and was a prominent landowner in the local community. She was a bright and pretty infant until calamity visited in the form of brain fever in 1882. The nineteen–month–old baby survived fortunately but was rendered blind, deaf and mute, a multiple curse that she transfigured into opportunity through iron determination.

In the initial years of disability, Keller struggled to express herself, 'giggling, chuckling, kicking and scratching' in unruly fashion. She formulated about sixty symbolic hand gestures to indicate what she wanted to her family. Refusing to admit her into a mental institution, her parents took her to meet Alexander Graham Bell who was devising hearing aids for the deaf. Her liveliness impressed Bell, who became a lifelong friend and benefactor. His conviction that she could learn social skills from a devoted private tutor led to the appointment of a young woman with limited eyesight, Anne Sullivan, as her home educator. Keller and Sullivan embarked on a monumental journey that had no precedent. The teacher treated Keller

as a normal girl without any trace of pity. The pupil showed an insatiable desire to learn words by spelling words on her palms, quickly mastering Braille script and square–hand writing. Her precocity for absorbing knowledge brought phenomenal results in just three years of training. By the end of 1887, the Perkins Institute for the Blind publicised her as 'One of the most remarkable children in existence.' Generous to the core, she capitalised on her fame to raise funds for rehabilitating a four–year–old handicapped boy.

In 1894, Keller moved to New York to acquire speech and hit it off with Mark Twain, the great novelist who pronounced her a 'Miracle girl'. Pursuing a college degree when most normal girls did not secure higher education, she enrolled at a preparatory school in Cambridge. Her fingertips bled from studying, but she gallantly cleared the tough admission tests for Radcliffe College in open competition with regular applicants. While acquiring a BA in language and philosophy, she wrote her awe–inspiring autobiography, The 'Story of My Life', which was translated into more than fifty languages. On graduating in 1904, her classmates eulogised, 'Beside her task, our efforts pale.'

In 1908, Keller's book, 'The World I Live In', described her techniques of perceiving the physical surroundings. Appointed to the Massachusetts Commission for the Blind, she highlighted the taboo subject of venereal diseases among prostitutes that caused blindness among their newborns. In 1909, she joined the Socialist Party and wrote a series of leftist essays, 'Out of the Dark' (1913). She pointed out the high incidence of blindness in the working class owing to industrial accidents and inadequate medical care. She supported women's suffrage and abortion, and favoured abolition of war, child labour, capital punishment etc. Keller's radical praise for the Russian revolution and black American organisations met heavy criticism, but her rebellious spirit went on. From 1914 onward, her diary was filled with public speaking invitations across the country and around the globe. Her world tours touched Japan, Egypt, Israel, South Africa, Australia and India, besides Europe and Latin America. Visiting schools and hospitals for blind children and soldiers, she brought cheer and compassion to those wallowing in despair. The massive amount of money raised from her lectures was donated to the American Foundation for the Blind. She also lobbied for legislation in the U.S. for uplifting the handicapped.

Keller's superstar image and intellectual reputation drew her into endorsements of particular American presidential candidates from 1924. She lent her name to letterheads of liberal organisations and her opinions attracted extensive press coverage. In 1927, she published 'My Religion', affirming a late religiosity that compensated her essentially isolated personal life. In her view, 'A spiritual world offers no difficulty to one who is deaf and blind.' She accorded music a special place in life, listening through vibrations that penetrated the floor and furniture. Her sense of smell was so well developed that friends teased her as an aromatic specialist.

In 1940, Keller's new book, 'Let Us Have Faith', iterated the mantra of overcoming debilitating barriers. Her optimism and idealistic outlook were best encapsulated in the statement: 'I seldom think about my limitations, and they never make me sad.' Her sang-froid, cheer and humour rubbed off on others and won her admirers among people everywhere. Keller's sheer charisma prompted several famous figures to leave written remembrances of her. On one visit to nuclear-devastated Hiroshima and Nagasaki, she stole many hearts by expressing the imperative to 'fight against the horrors of atomic warfare and for the constructive uses of atomic energy.'

Keller had reserves of superhuman gusto. Her last book, 'Teacher: Anne Sullivan Macy', hit the stands when she was 75. Old age compounded her discomfort in reviewing compositions, as assistants had to spell the words back into her hands. On her eightieth birthday, she told interviewers via interpreters, 'I will always, as long as I have breath, work for the handicapped.' She retained a child-like curiosity for happenings around her until the very end, even after retiring from public life in 1961 due to heart ailments.

In 1964, Keller was awarded the U.S. Presidential Medal of Freedom, crowning a most distinguished career in social service. In opinion polls at home and abroad, she swept the 'Greatest Woman' contest hands down. She shamed self-pitying defeatism and exhorted all human beings to determine their own fates. Helen Keller embodied character building that was easy to aspire to but Herculean to attain.

Right: that she could learn social skills from a devoted private tutor led to the appointment of a young woman with limited eyesight, Anne Sullivan, as her home educator. Keller and Sullivan embarked on a monumental journey that had no precedent. The teacher treated Keller as a normal girl without any trace of pity.

Diana, Princess of Wales

1961 – 1997

Fallen Princess

From the time of her engagement to the Prince of Wales in 1981 until her death in Paris in 1997, Diana was arguably the most famous woman in the world.

Diana, Princess of Wales, was the first wife of HRH The Prince Charles, Prince of Wales. Though she was noted for her pioneering charity work, the princess's philanthropic endeavours were overshadowed by a scandal–plagued marriage. Her bitter accusations of adultery, mental cruelty and emotional distress riveted the world for much of the 1980s and 1990s, spawning biographies, magazine articles and television movies.

Diana was a fashion icon, an ideal of feminine beauty, admired and emulated for her high–profile involvement in AIDS issues in Africa and the international campaign against landmines.

Charles and Diana had two children, William Arthur Philip Louis Windsor on June 21, 1982 and Henry Charles Albert David Windsor (commonly called Prince Harry) on September 15, 1984. After the birth of William, Diana suffered from post–natal depression. She later developed bulimia nervosa, and made a number of suicide attempts. In the mid 1980s her marriage fell apart, an event at first suppressed, but then sensationalised by, the world media. Both the Prince and Princess of Wales spoke to the press through friends, accusing each other of adultery. Charles resumed his relationship with Camilla Parker Bowles, after which Diana became involved with a series of men, including James Gilby, (the so–called Squidgygate affair). She later confirmed (in a television interview with Martin Bashir) that she had also had an affair with her riding instructor,

James Hewitt. Another of her lovers reportedly was a bodyguard assigned to the princess's security detail, although the princess adamantly denied a sexual relationship with him, as well as married art dealer Oliver Hoare.

The Prince and Princess of Wales separated on December 9, 1992; their divorce was finalised on August 28, 1996. The Princess lost the title of Her Royal Highness, and became Diana, Princess of Wales, a titular distinction befitting a divorced peeress.

On August 31, 1997 Diana was involved in a car accident in the Pont de l'Alma road tunnel in Paris, along with her romantic companion Dodi Al Fayed, their driver Henri Paul, and Al Fayed's bodyguard Trevor Rees–Jones.

Late in the evening of Saturday the 30th, Diana and Fayed departed the Hôtel Ritz in Place Vendome, Paris, and drove along the north bank of the Seine. Shortly after midnight on the 31st, their Mercedes–Benz S280 entered the underpass below the Place de l'Alma, pursued in various vehicles by nine French photographers and a motorcycle courier.

Dodi Al Fayed and Henri Paul were both declared dead at the scene of the crash. Trevor Rees–Jones was severely injured, but later recovered. Diana was freed, alive, from the wreckage, and after some delay due to attempts to stabilise her at the scene, she was taken by ambulance to Pitié–Salpêtrière Hospital shortly after 2:00 a.m.

Despite attempts to save her, her internal injuries were too extensive. Two hours later, at 4:00 that morning, the doctors pronounced her dead. Diana's death was greeted with extraordinary public grief. Diana, Princess of Wales is buried at Althorp in Northamptonshire on an island in the middle of a lake called the Round Oval.

Mother Teresa

1910 - 1997

A saint in her own lifetime

Born Agnes Gonxhe Bojaxhiu in Macedonia, Mother Teresa came from a well–to–do Albanian family. Her parents were Catholic, not Orthodox Christians as a majority of native Macedonians are.

Not much is known about Teresa's early life. What is known evolves from her own recollections – that she felt a strong, divine urge to work for the poor and the destitute when she was a teenager, which fuelled her energy to train for missionary work in India. When she was 18, Teresa arrived and joined the Sisters of Loreto, an Irish mission-ary community of nuns, in Calcutta, now Kolkata.

Following a short period of training, Teresa went to Darjeeling as a tyro sister. She took her first vows in 1931, and chose the name Sister Mary Teresa in honour of Teresa of Avila and Thérèse de Lisieux. When she took her final vows in 1937, she acquired the religious title, Mother Teresa. The rest is chiselled in immortal words in the annals of time.

Mother Teresa first taught at St Mary's High School in Kolkata; she became the institution's principal in 1944. Witness to abject poverty, she was moved. Two years later, she received a call from God 'To serve Him among the poorest of the poor.'

In 1948, Teresa received permission from the Vatican to become an independent nun. She left her school job, and enrolled for a short–term course with the Medical Mission Sisters in Bihar. She returned to Kolkata and lived with the Little Sisters of the Poor. It was, at this time, that she started an out–of–doors school for dispossessed children. Her work was quickly noticed and as volunteers joined her, she also began to receive financial help from church and government institutions.

The Vatican gave Teresa permission to start her own order in 1950. It was the beginning of the Missionaries of Charity whose duty was to care for 'The hungry, the naked, the homeless, the crippled, the blind, the lepers, and all those people who feel unwanted, unloved, uncar-ed for throughout society; people that have become a bur-den to society, and are shunned by everyone.' After a for-saken Hindu shrine was converted into the Kalighat Home for the Dying, a free hospice for the poor, Mother Teresa inaugurated another sanatorium, Nirmal Hriday, a home for lepers, Shanti Nagar (City of Peace), and an orphanage. Her selfless work began to appeal to people from all walks of life. Aid flowed by way of donations. By the 1960s, the Mother's Mission had hospital–clinics, orphanages and leper homes spread across the country.

HEROS & ICONS

▶ A saint in her own lifetime

Previous page: Not much is known about Teresa's early life. What is known evolves from her own recollections – that she felt a strong, divine urge to work for the poor and the destitute when she was a teenager, which fuelled her energy to train for missionary work in India.
Opposite: As Mother Teresa's health began to worry her, she suffered a heart attack in Rome, while visiting Pope John Paul II.

Pope Paul VI granted Mother Teresa permission to expand her order to other countries including Venezuela, Rome and Tanzania, and, thereafter to many countries across Asia, Africa and Europe, including Albania, and the U.S. Soon her inspired commitment stirred the conscience of millions worldwide to associate themselves with her order.

This led to the foundation of The Missionaries of Charity Brothers in 1963, and a contemplative branch of the Sisters in 1976. Just about anyone, with a missionary zeal, was welcomed by the Mother, who also started the Corpus Christi Movement for Priests in 1981.

Mother Teresa had become an international celebrity by the turn of the 1970s. She was a popular theme now captured on film, documentaries and books. She won the First Pope John XXIII Peace Prize in 1971. This was followed by a glut of awards including the Kennedy Prize (1971), the Nehru Prize for Promotion of International Peace and Understanding (1972), the Albert Schweitzer International Prize (1975), the Balzan Prize for Promoting Peace and Brotherhood Among Nations (1979), U.S. Presidential Medal of Freedom (1985), Congressional Gold Medal (1994), and Honourary Citizenship of the U.S. (1996).

Mother Teresa won the Nobel Prize in 1979. The Nobel citation eulogised her unparalleled contribution, thus: 'For work undertaken in the struggle to overcome poverty and distress, which also constitute a threat to peace.' When she was asked as to how one could promote world peace, she promptly replied: 'Go home and love your family.' She urged the Committee to do away with the $6,000 conventional ceremonial banquet so it could be given to the poor in Kolkata.

As Mother Teresa's health began to worry her, she suffered a heart attack in Rome, while visiting Pope John Paul II. A second attack came in 1989. This was followed by a bout of pneumonia and further heart complications. She had a pace–maker in her heart, but her frail frame was now not so willing, though her spirit was.

Mother Teresa fell and broke her collar–bone in 1997. This was soon followed by a spell of malaria, and failure of the left ventricle, for which she underwent heart surgery. She stepped down as Head of Missionaries of Charity. She died the same year at age 87. She was granted a full state funeral by a grateful nation and her adopted country.

In a tribute, the former U.N. Secretary–General Javier Pérez de Cuéllar, aptly said: 'She is the United Nations. She is peace in the world.'

Following Mother Teresa's death, the first step towards possible canonisation, or sainthood, was set in process. But, a miracle cure attributed to her suddenly turned controversial. Besides, there were questions asked on the funds and financial support she had received, and how they were spent, or not spent. There was variance too on her stand against abortion, and 'covert' conversion of Hindus and others to Christianity.

Mother Teresa's riposte to critics, when she was alive, was a simple, profound statement: 'No matter who says what, you should accept it with a smile and do your own work.' This she did without fear, prejudice or favour. Her work epitomised the Act of God. This was her greatness. A truly elevated, noble soul.

Mother Teresa is assured of her dignified place in human history. A true saint in her own lifetime.

Marilyn Monroe

1926 – 1962

The perpetual sex symbol

Marilyn Monroe, the perpetual sex symbol and pop emblem, was born Norma Jeane Mortensen in the charity ward of Los Angeles County Hospital. While her paternity has not been established, her mother, Gladys Monroe Baker, worked as a small time technician.

She was born in difficult times and Gladys was somehow able to find foster parents, the Bolender couple, for Marilyn. The religious Bolenders did not adopt her, but when Marilyn made and passed away into history, they claimed that they had sincerely thought of adopting her, but with Gladys' permission.

Gladys used to visit Marilyn, but never showed any tenderness toward her. Gladys lost her forbearing and was admitted to a mental hospital. After this, her good friend, Grace McKee, became Marilyn's custodian. When Grace married in 1935, Marilyn was sent to a Los Angeles Orphanage and several other foster homes, where she was ill–treated and uncared for.

When Grace did a volte–face and took her in her care, Marilyn married James Dougherty, the neighbour's son. Grace and her husband thought it would work for Marilyn, a teenager who had nobody to look up to. Quietly, Marilyn developed her acumen and drive that was instrumental in making her a star. She had a sharp, powerful mind, nothing short of analytical brilliance.

While her husband was away with the marines, a photographer captured her on film to boost army morale. Marilyn, with the consent of her in–laws, soon signed with a modelling firm. This led her to her first taste of studio activity with Twentieth Century Fox.

It was a Fox staffer that gave her a new name, Marilyn, which rhymed with her mother's maiden name, Monroe, who claimed but never proved to be a direct descendant of President James Monroe. Initially, Marilyn did not set the studio on fire. Destiny was manifest when she met Johnny Hyde, a partner of the William Morris Agency, in 1948. An old man, and married, Hyde fell head over heels for her allure.

It was his influence that helped Marilyn get roles in two films: 'The Asphalt Jungle' and 'All About Eve'.

Before Hyde had a fatal heart attack, he literally begged Marilyn to marry him, and promised that she would be a rich widow. She refused. When he died, Marilyn felt guilty for having hastened his end. The Hyde family threw her out of Hyde's Beverly Hills mansion. Distraught, Marilyn attempted to commit suicide, a day after Hyde's funeral.

▶ The perpetual sex symbol

Previous page: This was Marilyn, one of the most famous women that ever lived – one, who was not really understood beyond the glint of her extraordinary beauty. Opposite: Marilyn was found dead on August 5, 1962, in her bedroom, aged thirty–six. Her life was cut short by an overdose of sleeping pills.

Marilyn, a go–getter, pushed herself ahead and also posed nude. Hugh Hefner bought the rights to use the photographs for the first issue of his new men's magazine, 'Playboy' (1949). Fox was now certain that they had found a superstar in the making. But, Marilyn ripped up her contract and went to New York to hone her acting skills. She also formed her own production company with photographer Milton H. Greene. The movies she made were ridiculed. She now acquired a fresh contract with Fox that gave her freedom and allowed her to act in one movie, at least, under other banners. The first of them was 'Bus Stop'. Her co–stars now were all big names: Cary Grant, Clark Gable, Laurence Olivier, Tony Curtis et al. She also acted with Yves Montand which led to a sizzling affair.

Marilyn had several other affairs. Her fling with Joe Di Maggio, for one, was a complicated liaison with both blaming each other for infidelity. In 1956, Marilyn, after a strange courtship, married playwright Arthur Miller and soon after their return from England, found that she was pregnant. Her pregnancy was ectopic. An abortion was carried out to save her life. Sadly, a second pregnancy ended in miscarriage.

Two years later, Marilyn's life and marriage were in a shambles. Blame it on drugs and alcohol. Besides, she was not getting along well with Miller. A divorce was inevitable (1961). Meanwhile, Dougherty re–emerged and claimed that it was he who had made Marilyn a demi–goddess – a claim which fell flat. After her split with Miller, it was an encore for her affair with Di Maggio. By this time, though, her mental trauma was only expanding, and she had to undertake psychiatric treatment. Di

Maggio now took her to Columbia Presbyterian Hospital. But, true to being Marilyn, the explosive beauty was on prime time again, when she sang 'Happy Birthday Mr. President', at a televised birthday party for President John Kennedy with whom she was alleged to have had an affair in 1962.

Marilyn was found dead on August 5, 1962, in her bedroom, aged thirty–six. Her life was cut short by an overdose of sleeping pills. There were many theories about her death, the foremost among them being her close relationship with the 'Jinxed' Kennedy family. The analysis did not hold water. However, controversy still surrounds the circumstances that led Marilyn to her tragic end.

Although the Los Angeles County District Attorney came up with no realistic proof of villainy, two decades after her apparent suicide, it was Di Maggio who claimed her body and arranged her funeral. For twenty long years, Di Maggio religiously offered roses every second day of the week to her crypt. He kept himself absorbed in her memory. He never uttered a word about her nor did he attempt to write his memoirs.

It is said that Marilyn had once told her make–up man, Whitey Snyder, that she wanted him to make her up when she died. Snyder teased he sure would if Marilyn was still warm, not frozen.

This was Marilyn, one of the most famous women that ever lived – one, who was not really understood beyond the glint of her extraordinary beauty. She spawned a generation of women who followed in her every footstep imitating her charisma, fashion and style.

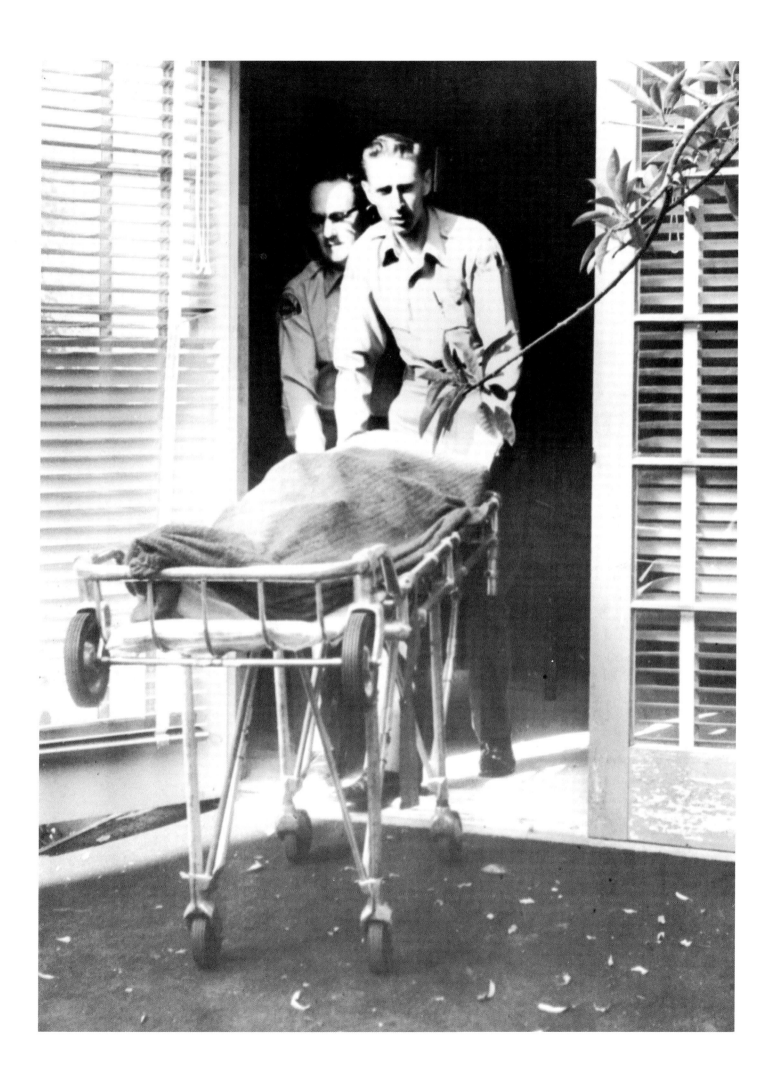

Edmund Hillary

1919 –

On top of the world

Edmund Percival Hillary, KG, ONZ, KBE is a New Zealander mountaineer and explorer, most famous for the first successful climb of Mount Everest. He reached the 29,035–foot (8850 m) summit on May 29, 1953 with Tenzing Norgay, a Sherpa.

Sir Edmund is the only living New Zealander to appear on a banknote. Born in Tuakau (south of Auckland), Hillary attended the Auckland Grammar School. The trip to school was over two hours each way, time which he spent reading. As he grew up he was smaller than his peers and very shy so he took refuge in his books and daydreams of a life filled with adventure.

At age 16, his interest in climbing was sparked during a school trip to Ruapehu. He found that his gangly and unco-ordinated frame was physically strong and had greater endurance than many of his tramping companions.

During World War II he was a RNZAF navigator. He was part of an unsuccessful New Zealand expedition to Everest in 1951 before joining the successful British attempt of 1953. He climbed 10 other peaks in the Himalaya on further visits in 1956, 1960–61 and 1963–65. He also reached the South Pole, as part of the British Commonwealth Trans–Antarctic Expedition, on January 4, 1958.

Edmund Hillary joined in Everest reconnaissance expeditions in 1951 and again in 1952. These exploits brought Hillary to the attention of Sir John Hunt, leader of an expedition sponsored by the Joint Himalayan Committee of the Alpine Club of Great Britain and the Royal Geographic Society to make the assault on Everest in 1953.

The expedition reached the South Peak in May, but all but two of the climbers who had come this far were forced to turn back by exhaustion at the high altitude. At last, Hillary and Tenzing Norgay, a native Nepalese climber who had participated in five previous Everest trips, were the only members of the party able to make the final assault on the summit.

At 11:30 on the morning of May 29, 1953, Edmund Hillary and Tenzing Norgay reached the summit, 29,028 feet above sea level, the highest spot on earth. As remarkable as the feat of reaching the summit, was the treacherous climb back down the peak.

Hillary has devoted much of his life to helping the Sherpa people of Nepal through the Himalayan Trust which he founded and to which he has given much of his time and energy. Through his efforts he has succeeded in building many schools and hospitals in this remote region of the Himalaya. He has stated that he regards this as his most important achievement. He is also the Honourary President of the American Himalayan Foundation, a U.S. non–profit body that also helps improve the ecology and living conditions in the Himalayas.

To mark the occasion of the 50th anniversary of the first successful ascent of Everest, the Nepalese Government conferred honourary citizenship upon Sir Edmund at a special golden jubilee celebration in the capital Kathmandu. Sir Edmund is the first foreign national to receive such an honour from the Nepalese.

Sir Edmund's life was darkened by the loss of his wife and daughter in a plane crash in 1975. He later remarried and continues to occupy himself with worldwide environmental causes.

Coco Chanel

1883 – 1971

Fashion icon

Born Gabrielle Chanel in 1883 in Saumur, France, 'Coco' Chanel opened her first boutique in 1912 and quickly became the premier fashion designer in Paris. Chanel replaced the uncomfortable corsets and evening wear of the period with simple, elegant clothing including dresses, trousers for women and suits. The Chanel brand is still the most famous with merchandise including fabric, perfumes, jewellery and accessories.

Chanel was brought up in poor conditions and with the death of her mother when she was just six, she was moved to the care of relatives – abandoned by her father. Chanel took on the persona of Coco when she decided to become a cafe singer during a brief period between 1905 and 1908.

Chanel was raised in a French orphanage. The simplistic and stark dress of the nuns and their environment influenced Chanel's designs. Her simple little black dresses, squarish suits, and almost boyish suits were vastly divergent from the confining and tight–fitting corsets and long dresses with petticoats. By the mid '20s, Chanel's comfortable and practical designs flourished and she opened two boutiques: one in Paris and the other in Biarritz. Together these shops employed over 300 people. Chanel befriended wealthy aristocrat Arthur Capel and used his resources to set up the new and thriving business.

Chanel had a strategic mind and her future was the most important factor in her life. Now, with a large list of regular customers mainly made up of celebrities and women of society, Chanel was able to expand her business successfully using her trademark hats to promote her label.

By 1920, Chanel's fashion empire had grown considerably. She launched her now famous perfume Chanel No. 5 onto the world market along with her business partner Pierre Wertheimer whose family still controls the perfume company. Her relaxed style of fashion had now become a world–wide phenomenon and her creations were in great demand.

Chanel was the perfect model for her own styles – dressing in clothing that were in sharp contrast to popular fashion in past decades. Chanel appeared in society and attended functions to be seen and talked about. In 1931, Chanel was paid over a million dollars by Samuel Goldwin to dress his stars including Katharine Hepburn, Grace Kelly and Elizabeth Taylor. However, many movie stars refused to work with her and she had no option but to return to her shops in France until the situation and attitudes in Hollywood changed after the war.

Nazi occupation of France in the 1940s meant the fashion business in Paris suffered for many years. Chanel's affair during World War II with a Nazi officer resulted in some years of diminished popularity and an exile to Switzerland. In 1954 her comeback restored her to the first ranks of haute couture. Her natural, casual clothing including the Chanel suit once again received world attention.

Chanel was still working in 1971 when she died. Fashion supremo Karl Lagerfeld has been chief designer of Chanel's fashion house since 1983 and he has embraced her style and carried it through almost three decades with her timeless and classic suits, shoes and accessories incorporating modern designs with the already established classic look.

Coco Chanel was an icon in the fashion industry – she was passionate about clothing design and a trendsetter whose influence can still be seen today.

Jesse Owens

1913 – 1980

A great sportsman

James Cleveland Owens was born in a small town in Alabama to Henry and Emma Owens. When he was eight, his parents decided to migrate to Cleveland, Ohio. They were not wealthy and all Jesse's father hoped for was a steady, better job.

Owens came to fame in Berlin in 1936. The world was witness to a phenomenal blast of speed, guts, stamina and the calm courage of a young, strong twenty–three–year–old black athlete from the U.S., in the Olympic Games held at the zenith of Nazi supremacy to demonstrate the superiority of the Aryan, 'Master' race. While Adolf Hitler, supremo of the Third Reich, watched the proceedings, in spectacular regalia, Jesse Owens, a member of the 'Inferior' race, created a sensation by winning a then–unparalleled four gold medals, and, with that, a permanent place in sporting history.

For Owens, who had set the river Danube aflame, the whole drama was just a simple encore. Because, only a year earlier, Jesse had set six World records which also included the 100–yard long jump, 220–yard, and 200m hurdles within a space of 45 minutes, while he was troubled with an injured back! What's more, for a man who once beat a race-horse in a 100–yard sprint, the golds at Berlin were all achieved in a day's work. A truly Olympian feat.

Owens' first tryst with glory was the 100m sprint. He won it in a canter, by equalling an existing World record time of 10.03 seconds. The second medal was annexed in the long jump event, as Owens skied to a crescendo with a giant leap of 26 feet, or 8.64m.

Jesse had 'fouled' on his first two jumps, and only managed to romp home off his third and final try, in the qualifying round, which was ruled as 'Okay' by officials. In his second attempt, Jesse's toes had kissed the bank of earth encircling the take–off board. One last chance remained. It was at this stage, that Lutz Long, Germany's number one and Owens' most serious challenger for the title, walked up to his American rival and advised him to place a towel before the take–off mark. The idea worked. The rest is history, a silver–lining and triumph of sporting spirit over competition.

Jesse's third gold came in the 200m race, with a new Olympic record timing of 20.07 seconds, which, incidentally, also made him the first since the turn of the last century to win three individual golds in the globe's premier sports event. Television cameras were in action for the first time ever at the Olympics and captured some great images for posterity,

Jesse, the poor black boy, was on top of the world. While Hitler waved his hand in admiration, what was most shameful was the eerie silence of the White House and U.S. government, juxtaposed by shoddy coverage in the American media. Worse still, Atlanta Constitution, a liberal newspaper, did not carry a single picture of Owens. In sharp contrast, the German press was chock–a–block. for a sporting hero. All thanks to propaganda and Nazi Germany's extreme flair for details: 'Care should be taken not to offend Negro athletes.'

If Charles Riley, a white American, his school coach, made Jesse realise his vast potential, Owens' wife, Minnie, was another person, who stood like a pillar behind her husband's ups and downs: serene, unwavering. And, she shared Jesse's wonderful philosophy too – that they were Americans first; blacks, next. This is the legacy of Owens: a great sportsman, individual and a jewel among men.

Jacqueline Kennedy Onassis

1929 – 1994

Legacy of charm and grace

Born into an elitist New York family and society, Jacqueline, or Jackie, was the eldest daughter of John Vernou Bouvier III, a flamboyant stockbroker and Janet Norton Lee, who herself was a high–flying banker's daughter.

Jacqueline's father was of French descent. Jackie's younger sister Caroline was married three times: on all occasions to high–class family scions. The Bouvier sisters also descended, through their natural family tree, from a merchant family of Dutch–African ancestry that settled in New Amsterdam in the late 17th century.

Jacqueline won her first academic feathers as the 'Debutante of the Year' in 1947-48. Educated at Miss Porter's School, Vassar College and George Washington University, she also spent time pursuing her academic interests in France. Not surprisingly, Jacqueline spoke French effortlessly.   That she had a special taste for languages was borne by the fact that she could speak Spanish just as fluently.

Jacqueline was engaged to stock agent John Husted, Jr., but she, by a whim of providence and also choice married Senator John F. Kennedy, one of the Democratic Party's rising stars, and future U.S. Presidents, in September 1953. Not that it was sudden romance that did her in – when in Washington Jackie was an 'Inquisitive photographer' for a local newspaper. Her job once took her to Senator Kennedy, a charismatic eligible bachelor. Their relationship progressed quietly and leisurely Unlike their wedding which heightened public hype on a national scale. The couple had four children: Arabella, who was stillborn in 1956; Caroline Bouvier Kennedy, the following year; John Fitzgerald Kennedy Jr., (1960–1999), who died in a tragic plane crash; and Patrick Bouvier Kennedy, who did not live on after his birth in August 1963.

When Kennedy beat Richard Nixon by a whisker in the 1960 presidential elections, and became the 35th President of the U.S. in 1961, Jacqueline became one of the youngest First Ladies in history. She brought splendour, acumen, and refined tang. She also stimulated an interest in American culture never before incarnate at the White House. She made the White House into a museum, an emblem of U.S. history.

At the crest of the Kennedy era, Jackie was sitting next to her husband when he was assassinated. The fateful day was November 22, 1963 in Dallas, Texas. In the terrible commotion that followed, Jackie held her nerve. She climbed to the left–centre back of the limousine shaft, behind and left of John's lifeless body, and quickly picked

▶ Legacy of charm and grace

Previous page: Jackie was a talented, intelligent lady. She could judge people well. She had a flair for words and writing and made a good editor at Doubleday in her later years.
Opposite: Jackie did not appear in public for one year following John's assassination; she was in mourning. However, she made just one appearance during a mass at St. Matthew's Cathedral in Washington that marked what would have been her husband's 47th birthday.

up a piece of her husband's head, which was ripped off by the tracer bullet. The whole of America and the rest of the world were shocked and dismayed – a leader of rare charisma and hope was gone.

Jackie was able to bring herself together in the midst of desolation and personal agony. She planned her husband's funeral, with the active involvement of the army. A picture of gallant courage during the funeral, Jackie won the heart of millions of people all over the world. This infringed upon her privacy and the image of the black–veiled widow mourning for her gunned down husband and U.S. President was freeze–framed in history.

As she held her two children, one in each hand, and crouched on her knees at the bier and lit the eternal flame at her husband's grave at Arlington National Cemetery, the scene was not just poignant and sombre, but also heart–rending. As the London Evening Standard observed: 'Jacqueline Kennedy has given the American people one thing they have always lacked: majesty.'

Jackie did not appear in public for one year following John's assassination; she was in mourning. However, she made just one appearance during a mass at St. Matthew's Cathedral in Washington that marked what would have been her husband's 47th birthday.

Circumstances once again rocked her existence, when her former brother–in–law Robert F. Kennedy was assassinated. Jackie got this nagging feeling that the Kennedys were 'Under attack' and also jinxed. She also felt that she and her children were in danger. She decided that it was time to move away from the U.S..

In October 1968, three months after Robert's assassination, Jackie married Aristotle Onassis, a Greek–shipping magnate, in Skorpios. She was no longer eligible for Secret Service Security. However, Jackie's marriage to Onassis made sense to her. Onassis had the clout to provide the safeguard she wanted. There was another advantage. The wedding also gave Onassis the social hoard and respectability, the rich man himself craved, so much so he abruptly ended his affair with Maria Callas, an opera diva.

The marriage was all glamour; it was not something that was built on love. The couple seldom spent time together. That Onassis made friends with Caroline and John, Jr. was the only saving grace. But, Jackie never ever got on well with her step–daughter Christina and preferred shopping to becoming a housewife. When Onassis died in March 1975, he bequeathed a vast fortune to Jackie.

There had also been more than a brace of embarrassments for the Kennedy family during the Jackie–Onassis honeymoon of luxury. To cull one example: a paparazzo had photographed Jackie nude on a Greek island. Larry Flynt, the publisher of *Hustler*, who had bought the photos, published them in the magazine's August 1975 issue.

Jackie was a talented, intelligent lady who could judge people well. She had a flair for words and writing and made a good editor at Doubleday in her later years. She also lived in New York City, at this time, and Martha's Vineyard. In the process, she stirred up a hornet's nest by living with Maurice Tempelsman, a Belgian–born industrialist and diamond merchant, a married man.

Jackie, Princess Charming in her prime, was diagnosed with cancer in 1994. She died in her sleep at age 64 but she left behind a legacy of charm and grace that carries on to this day in every sense of her being.

Pelé
1940 –

A quintessential genius

Former Brazilian football player, Pelé is rated by many to be the greatest player of all time – with the possible exception of Diego Maradona. He was born Edson Arantes do Nascimento.

An extremely versatile footballer, and an equally successful goal scorer, Pelé was highly skilled at dribbling and passing. He also possessed great defensive skills for a striker.

Pelé started his football career in Santos in 1956, aged 15. He played in his first international match within a year. He stayed with Santos, the club that made him famous, for his entire career. In 1958, Pelé, at age 17, became the youngest–ever World Cup winner in Sweden. He played for two more Brazilian World Cup–winning teams (1962 and 1970). Pelé played for his country in four World Cup's with immense passion, commitment, flair and purpose.

Pelé showed a remarkably natural penchant for football. He zoomed into fame at an early age. He came from a poor family, but success and riches followed him wherever he went. His love for the world's greatest sport made him a colossus; however, his profound interest and compassion for Brazil's underprivileged children remained firm.

Until his farewell game in 1977, Pelé appeared in 1,363 first–class matches, including 111 internationals. His tally: 1,300 goals. That he helped Brazil win the World Cup in Sweden with two fantastic goals stands tall in his roster of achievements.

For an average–sized man, Pelé was blessed with speed, great balance, tremendous visualisation, the ability to control the ball splendidly, and the facility to shoot powerfully and accurately with either foot or head. He was also a brilliant reader of the game. He could decipher its every nuance in his mind. He once admitted that his skills were God–given. God could not, of course, play football. Hence, he gave what he wanted to Pelé. Pelé's very presence brought magic to the game – something that no other player could dream, or think of.

When Pelé started playing the game in the U.S. in 1975, football was just a spectator sport. With a fabulous $4.75 million three–year contract, Pelé came out of retirement and transformed the game. He gave American football a new high a newly found respectability. Attendance began to soar in every stadium he played.

Long after Pelé hung up his boots, his name continues to be a religion in Brazil. He is seen as a God, not just king. Pelé has been Brazil's best ambassador and advertisement. He has been equally spirited in social causes too and has promoted products such as clothes, vitamins, batteries, and real estate. He has never ever sold his name to advertisements for alcohol, cigarettes and cigars. What has also been unique is that the richest Brazilian of his generation, has invested over seventy per cent of his fortune in his own country. He has maintained a clean image, despite a flutter or two of the heart for a maiden, when it was least expected.

How does Pelé reflect on all the glory, and adulation, that surround him today? Simple. With quiet dignity and plainness. In his own words: 'One thing is certain. I will never stop thinking of God for every wonderful thing He has granted me. If a man would try to make more daily contact with God, the world would be a less aggressive place to live in.'

It sums up Pelé – a quintessential genius, the greatest–ever of his type to play football, and an equally great human being.

Estée Lauder

1906 – 2004

Cosmetic pioneer

Estée lauder founded the international cosmetics empire in 1946 that still bears her name today.

In the initial stages she had only a limited range of products: a cream for blemished skin, a cleansing oil and an assortment of makeup. After orders came flooding in from Saks of Fifth Avenue in New York she and her husband Joseph spent hours cooking up creams and lotions, utilising the formulae devised by her uncle, a chemist who created face creams in his backyard laboratory. This was to launch her career on a grand scale. Lauder was one of the first to use sampling as a marketing technique, offering women a chance to try the product before buying it, and she used a personal selling approach that proved to be a powerful example for her skin care range.

Utilising the talents of her uncle the couple came up with the formulation of their original product line; Estée Lauder Créme Pack, cleansing oil and the All Purpose Créme and skin lotion.

In 1953 she launched Youth Dew, a bath oil scent that could also be used as a perfume. This product Youth Dew, greatly influenced the popularity of perfume at the time, selling fifty thousand units in the first year. By 1984, sales rose to one hundred and fifty million. Initially marketed to housewives, the homemaker who could only afford an occasional luxury, and priced at $8.50 a bottle, it was a great success and caused a sensation. Later she introduced many popular perfumes including Azuree, Aliage, Private Collection, White Linen and Beautiful. Always wary of competitors, only trusted family members knew the formulas for the various fragrances.

After the initial success at Saks, Estée Lauder marketed to the high end department stores where they are still sold today. By the 60s Estée Lauder was a world wide corporation selling their products in London and opening outlets across Europe and Asia.

In 1964 Lauder established one of the first male fragrance lines, Aramis for Men, which included an entire range of men's skincare products that were to revolutionise the industry once more.

Yet another of her innovations was to launch a fragrance–free skin care line, Clinique, which is as popular today as it was then.

In addition to numerous cosmetic industry accolades, Lauder received several awards including the French government's insignia of Chevalier of the Legion of Honour in 1978 and the gold medal award by the city of Paris in 1979. She also received the crystal apple from the Association for a Better New York and the Albert Einstein College of Medicine Spirit of Achievement award in 68. This was particularly ironic due to France being the most difficult market for Lauder initially to enter.

In 1970 she was recognised as one of America's most Outstanding Women in Business. During the 1960s, 70s, 80s and 90s, the Lauder corporation brought in new products and acquired companies including Prescriptives, Origins, M.A.C, Bobbi Brown, Donna Karan, Aveda and La Mer.

In 1973 Estée Lauder stepped down as president and became a chairman of the board while still having an important role in the creative aspect of the company. The business was privately owned up until 1995.

Estée Lauder died on April 24, 2004 of cardiopulmonary failure at her home in New York at the age of 97.

She will be remembered for her courageous business ethics and as the pioneer and face of cosmetics.

Pope John Paul II

1920 – 2005

Servant of God

His Holiness Pope John Paul II was born Karol Józef Wojty and reigned as Pope of the Roman Catholic Church and sovereign of Vatican City for almost 27 years, from 16 October 1978 until his death.

He was the first non–Italian to serve in office since the Dutch–German Pope Adrian VI died in 1523. John Paul II's reign was the third–longest in the history of the Papacy, after those of Saint Peter (about 35 years) and Blessed Pius IX (31 years). This is in a distinctive contrast with that of his predecessor Pope John Paul I, who died suddenly after only 33 days in office, and in whose memory John Paul II named himself.

The reign was marked by a continuing decline of Catholicism in industrialised nations and expansion in the third world.

Pope John Paul II emphasised what he called the universal call to holiness and attempted to define the Catholic Church's role in the modern world. He spoke out against ideologies and politics of communism, imperialism, relativism, materialism, fascism (including nazism), racism and unrestrained capitalism. In many ways, he fought against oppression, secularism and poverty.

Although he was on friendly terms with many Western heads of state and leading citizens, he reserved a special opprobrium for what he believed to be the corrosive spiritual effects of modern Western consumerism and the concomitant widespread secular and hedonistic orientation of Western populations.

He affirmed, explained and defined Catholic teachings on life by opposing abortion, contraception, capital punishment, embryonic stem–cell research, human cloning, euthanasia, war and accepted evolution. He also defended traditional teachings on marriage and gender roles by opposing divorce, same–sex marriage and the ordination of women. He called upon Catholics to vote according to their beliefs, even if they were based on their religion and suggested that politicians who strayed be denied the eucharist.

John Paul became known as the 'Pilgrim Pope' for having travelled greater distances than had all his predecessors combined.

It is reported that as of October 2004, he had beatified 1,340 people, more people than any previous pope. The Vatican asserts he canonised more people than the combined tally of his predecessors during the last five centuries, and from a far greater variety of cultures. Whether he had canonised more saints than all previous popes put together, as is sometimes also claimed, is difficult to prove, as the records of many early canonisations are incomplete, missing or inaccurate. However, it is known that his abolition of the office of Promoter Fidei (Promoter of the Faith, a.k.a. Devil's Advocate) streamlined the canonisation process.

Pope John Paul II died on 2 April 2005 after a long fight against Parkinson's disease and other illnesses. Immediately after his death, many of his followers demanded that he be elevated to sainthood as soon as possible, shouting 'Santo Subito'. Both L'Osservatore Romano and Pope Benedict XVI, Pope John Paul II's successor, referred to John Paul II as 'great.' Six weeks later, on May 13, Pope Benedict formally opened the cause for beatification for his predecessor, which now allows Catholics to refer to Pope John Paul as 'Servant of God.'

John Paul was succeeded by the Dean of the College of Cardinals, Joseph Cardinal Ratzinger of Germany, the former head of the Congregation for the Doctrine of the Faith who had led the funeral mass for John Paul.

Desmond Tutu

1931 –

Champion of the oppressed

A rchbishop Desmond Mpilo Tutu was the Martin Luther King of South Africa, a servant of God who championed the rights of the oppressed in every corner of the globe. The first leader to popularise the anti–apartheid movement of South Africa in front of world audiences, he reified the venerable Christian tradition of struggling for human rights of the helpless. To him went the credit of articulating that opposition to evil systems was a moral duty of the conscientious.

Tutu was born of a Xhosa schoolteacher and Tswana domestic servant in Klerksdorp, the gold and mineral–rich part of Transvaal. His middle name 'Mpilo' meant life, received from his grandmother because of the child's frailty and forebodings that he would not survive. Though baptised as a Methodist, young Tutu's family changed denomination en masse to Anglicanism. He studied at mission schools at which his father taught and mother cooked.

At the age of twelve, Tutu was initiated into compassion when he noticed blind students being admirably assisted in a school. He hero–worshipped the British anti–apartheid Bishop Trevor Huddleston, who lived amongst the poorest slum dwellers of Sophiatown in

Johannesburg. Tutu was moved by Huddleston's humility and lack of racial bias. When Huddleston greeted Tutu's mother respectfully, he was wonderstruck: 'I couldn't believe it– a white man raising his hat to a simple black labouring woman.' Huddleston visited him in hospital when he was recovering from tuberculosis.

Teenaged Tutu sold peanuts at suburban railway stations and caddied on golf courses for pocket money. Though interested in studying medicine after high school, familial poverty forced him to take a diploma and bachelor's degree in teaching. From 1954 to 1957, he taught in Johannesburg schools, but resigned in disgust when the apartheid regime introduced a second–class 'Bantu education' system. For practical economic reasons and in the hope of finding a 'Likely means of service', Tutu turned to theological studies in seminaries of Huddleston's order. Only later would he recall that when he stood at crossroads, he was 'Grabbed by God by the scruff of the neck.' Serious religious education burnished him into a spiritually motivated idealistic man.

Ordained as an Anglican parish priest in 1961, Tutu lectured in Benoni and Alberton. When an opportunity arose, he moved to London to obtain a masters level degree in theology. He taught in the independent African enclave of

▶ Champion of the oppressed

Previous page: A servant of God, Tutu championed the rights of the oppressed in every corner of the globe. Opposite: It was Tutu's mass march with church leaders in 1990 that opened the floodgates of liberalisation by F.W. de Klerk's government, heralding the beginning of the end of apartheid.

Lesotho and travelled to several other parts of Africa and Asia on behalf of the World Council of Churches, where he was Assistant Director between 1972 and 1975. Tutu's diligence, ecclesiastical passion and administrative acumen propelled his rise within church institutions.

In 1975, Tutu was appointed the first black Anglican dean of Johannesburg. He utilised his inviolable position and personal integrity to attack the injustices of apartheid and excesses in the black reaction to it. Non–violence was Tutu's unofficial middle name. He attempted to channel the seething rage of black youth into peaceful demonstrations and wrote to the Prime Minister to deal with their problems. The authorities did not pay heed to the warning of this 'Troublemaker' and it resulted in the infamous Soweto riots of 1976.

In 1978, Tutu became the first black Secretary General of the South African Council of Churches (SACC), transforming it into an important outlet for black protest while the African National Congress (ANC) and other political outfits were banned. He denounced the government's forced resettlement of urban blacks as akin to Hitler's 'Final solution' for Jews and characterised racial discrimination 'As evil as Nazism.' His theological criticism of apartheid as a heresy and apostasy made him a hate figure for conservative whites.

In trips to the U.S. and U.K. in 1981, he repeated the appeal for economic embargo, defying the wrath of the Pretoria government. Tutu's passport was confiscated and a governmental commission investigated SACC for foreign influences and economic sabotage. He went on undeterred, aware of the value of mobilising western media and civil society behind the anti–apartheid banner.

In 1984, Tutu was awarded the Nobel Peace Prize. He donated the prize money for education of indigent South African black students. In 1985, he was installed as Bishop of Johannesburg. The following year, he reached the pin-

nacle of church hierarchy as the Archbishop of Cape Town. As South Africa bled under martial law, Tutu launched successful personal interventions to save the lives of mourners and imprisoned labour agitators.

Unlike the ANC, Tutu was a stickler for peaceful means and deplored black–on–black violence. Once, he risked his own life to rescue an alleged police informer from being burnt by a black mob. He decried 'Necklace lynching' in black townships and employed Gandhian emotional blackmail by threatening to leave South Africa if the practice was not halted.

In 1988, Tutu formed the Committee for Defence of Democracy to evade the official restriction on anti–apartheid organisations. He met ANC leaders in exile and coordinated positions with them at several historic junctures. It was Tutu's mass march with church leaders in 1990 that opened the floodgates of liberalisation by F.W. de Klerk's government, heralding the beginning of the end of apartheid.

In 1994, President Nelson Mandela made an 'Inspired choice' by appointing Tutu head of the Truth and Reconciliation Commission (TRC) to secure moral reparations for apartheid–era excesses. TRC staff testified that Tutu was the indispensable captain of their experimental ship, a guide and compass without whom the ghosts of the past could not be exorcised. He conducted himself as a 'Wounded healer' who cared deeply for victims and perpetrators.

Tutu's speeches and spiritual discourses connected the microphone to his inner voice. His pulpit oratory electrified audiences with witticisms and parables. An animated priest, he yelped, giggled and danced during sermons, whooping with congregations. Laughter and joy were integral to his vision of making forgiveness a pillar of practical politics.

Jesse Jackson

1941 -

Equality and justice

Reverend Jesse Louis Jackson was at the forefront of social justice and equality causes in the U.S. for more than three decades. His life was an indefatigable search for empowerment of the second–class citizen. He strove to change the internal and external policies of the world's most powerful country. His national and international reputation as a champion of the downtrodden and suppressed was second to none among African Americans by the late Twentieth Century.

Jackson was born in Greensville, South Carolina, into a socio–economic cauldron that definitively shaped his life's calling. He was the product of a teenage pregnancy, an illegitimate child whose biological father refused to acknowledge paternity. His mother was a poor maid and beautician who struggled to make ends meet. Years later, Jackson would proudly proclaim, 'Though I was born in a slum, the slum wasn't born in me.' Jackson's tireless efforts to promote self–esteem among America's underdogs came from the inner need to come to terms with his own origins.

Brought up in the stifling environment of racial segregation, Jackson was a star football player in his all–black high school and President of the local Future Teachers of America. Jackson's early sensitivity to racial insults about black students' academic backwardness led to future commitments to educational improvement of minorities. His leadership abilities blossomed in college, when he joined the 'Sit-in' movements protesting racial discrimination in restaurants, libraries and public spaces.

Awarded a degree in sociology in 1963, Jackson worked for the Young Democrats Convention and the Democratic governor of his state. A deeply religious man, he joined the Chicago Theological Seminary. Motivated to bolster Dr. Martin Luther King Jr.'s voting rights march in Alabama, he left the Seminary in 1965 and took to a career in politics from which there was no looking back.

Jackson was at the centre of the major civil rights organisations of the 1960s, collaborating closely with Dr. King. In 1966, the latter appointed him Executive Director of Operation Breadbasket, a programme to find employment for blacks in firms having heavy minority patronage. Dr. King was concerned about Jackson's need for the limelight, but was impressed with his mobilisation skills.

Jackson's enigmatic personality contained the incompatible mix of altruism and one–upmanship. A rising star in black America's firmament, he set sights on inheriting his mentor's mantle after Dr. King's assassination in 1968. His clever usage of the media to anoint himself as

► Equality and justice

Previous page: Jesse Jackson was at the forefront of social justice and equality causes in the U.S. for more than three decades.
Opposite: Jackson was adept at orchestrating media events and garnering publicity for his cause and for himself.

Dr.King's rightful heir created the impression of an ego-centric and dangerously selfish person. Jackson's ambitious self–aggrandising behaviour earned him many enemies within Dr. King's circle and ultimately led to his ouster from the Southern Christian Leadership Conference.

In 1971, with fanfare and celebrity attendance, Jackson formed his own national organisation– PUSH (People United to Serve Humanity). PUSH's projects of job training, voter registration, business enterprise development etc. for minorities brought Jackson to national attention. He visited scores of schools across America to inspire young blacks to reject drugs, switch off television and study doggedly. Gifted with the gab and a preaching style of stirring oratory, Jackson instilled in young blacks a sense of dignity that they would never forsake. His famous school chant emancipated thousands: 'I am somebody. I may be poor, but I am somebody. Respect me. My mind is a pearl. I can learn anything. I am somebody.'

Jackson emerged as the most persuasive black leader and was respected as a legitimate voice on minority issues by the press and in government. Influenced by the anti–war wave after Vietnam, he gained a worldwide reputation for humanist and anti–militarist standpoints. He was a brilliant negotiator and diplomat who went on several foreign jaunts to break deadlocks and mediate conflicts. A powerful behind–the–scenes presence in international politics, he helped release an American pilot from Syrian custody in 1983; obtained the freedom of fourty eight Cuban–American prisoners and persuaded Fidel Castro to attend church in 1984; promulgated peace plans for South Africa, Central America and the Middle East; freed 500 hostages held by Saddam Hussein in Kuwait in 1991, and repeated the feat in Bosnia (1999) and Sierra Leone (2000).

In 1984 and 1988, Jackson unsuccessfully ran for the Democratic nomination for the U.S. Presidency, fulfilling the aspiration of Dr. King and breaking the psychological barrier that occluded blacks from seeking high office. His 'Rainbow Coalition' ticket in 1988 brought together workers, farmers, blacks, Hispanics, Asians, Jews, Christians, Native Americans, homosexuals and white liberals, an unprecedented challenge to 'Reaganomic' hegemony. 'My constituency', he thundered, 'Is the desperate, the damned, the disinherited, the disrespected, and the despised.' Jackson's strategy was to unify the wretched of the earth and usher in an order based on justice and moral values. 'The Search for Common Ground', a book written by a black theologian, guided him on this voyage.

Jackson was adept at orchestrating media events and garnering publicity for his cause and for himself. He delivered some of the most spellbinding ad–lib speeches in American history. His instinct for the right phrase, the repartee that makes headlines and the crowd–pleasing dramatic gesture marked a real professional in public relations. His call to 'Choose the human race over the nuclear race' and his metaphor of America as a 'Multicultural quilt' turned into household sound–bytes.

Like Dr. King, Jackson identified unequal economic relationships as the underlying cause of racial discrimination. In 2000, he authored 'It's About the Money', a book of financial advice for African Americans. He canvassed for increasing black power on Wall Street and forced major multinational corporations to defenestrate racial biases.

The most powerful African American leader since the 1970s, Jackson was mired in controversies. His imperious mannerisms provoked accusations of megalomania and narcissism from detractors. However, none could gainsay his vision of an alternative America that 'Ought to be.'

Martin Luther King Jr.

1929 – 1968

Civil rights activist

D r. Martin Luther King, Jr., the legendary African–American civil rights activist, was one of the most noteworthy leaders in U.S. history. He was a man of many parts: a hero, peace-maker and martyr. His name stands tall in con-temporary history of non–violence.

King became the pastor of the Dexter Avenue Baptist Church in Montgomery, Alabama, in the early 1950s. He was a leader of the Montgomery Bus Boycott (1955), a campaign which began when Rosa Parks refused to vacate her seat to a white man. King was arrested during this movement. His challenge resulted with a U.S. Supreme Court edict which outlawed racial discrimination on intra–state buses.

King organised and led marches for the right to vote, desegregation, fair hiring, and other basic civil rights. His humane spirit and enterprise bore fruit. They were suc-cessfully formulated into U.S. law, especially with the pas-sage of the Civil Rights Act and Voting Rights Act (1965). In October 1964, King became the youngest recipient of the Nobel Peace Prize.

King came from a black, Southern religious family. An outstanding student, he gave up his early interests in med-icine and law to enter the ministry on his father's insis-tence. Soon, King became fully conversant with Gandhi. He rose to prominence acquainted with and influenced by theology and Gandhian philosophy of non–violence.

King was a non–violent revolutionary, a personification of the most powerful force for the long overdue social, political, and economic reconstruction of America and the world. But, for those in charge of U.S. intelligence, the mil-itary, and law enforcement, King's active opposition to the Vietnam War, and his campaign for the poor, not just blacks and moderate whites, constituted a grave threat to U.S. stability and society, a society which was already rife with unrest. Some also mistook King for a communist.

When the civil rights movement was gaining ground, Martin Luther King said: 'We have no alternative but to protest. For many years, we have shown an amazing patience. We have sometimes given our white brothers the feeling that we liked the way we were being treated. But, we have come here tonight to be saved from that patience that makes us patient with anything less than freedom and justice.'

King laid the groundwork for the organisation, the Southern Christian Leadership Conference in 1957 at a time when his name was making waves. He was elected its president. Soon, he began helping other communities

▶ Civil rights activist

Previous page: When more than 200,000 people gathered in the shadow of the Lincoln Memorial during what was civil rights activists' historic march to Washington DC, on August 28, 1963, King using biblical phraseology, emphasised his faith that all men would someday be brothers. Opposite: King died a martyr. Yet, in the face of the bullet that took his life, his deep faith and belief that truth and justice would one day triumph, remained firm and unshakeable.

organise their own protests against racial discrimination and injustice. King's visit to India in 1959 was another turning point. He was given a rousing welcome fit for a President in New Delhi. His belief in non–violence was further strengthened. He returned to the U.S. to become co–pastor, with his father, of Ebenezer Baptist Church.

Three years later, his non–violent tactics were put to the ultimate test in Birmingham, during a mass protest for fair hiring practices and the desegregation of department store facilities. Constabulary cruelty used against the marchers embossed the troubles of blacks to the country with stunning effect. King had won Round One. The authorities arrested him; they could, however, not apprehend his firm resolve.

When more than 200,000 people gathered in the shadow of the Lincoln Memorial during what was civil rights activists' historic march to Washington DC, on August 28, 1963, King using biblical phraseology, emphasised his faith that all men would someday be brothers. It was part of his celebrated 'I have a dream' speech. The rest as the saying goes is part of history – a part of humanity's sojourn in its war against racial oppression.

King believed that non–violent resistance was the most powerful weapon available to end subjugation and win freedom. He was as popular a figure in America's struggle for equality as Gandhi during India's crusade for independence from British rule. However, there was a tinge of impatience in the ranks of his movement.

The first sign of opposition from within the movement came into the open in March 1965. King's last–minute decision to back out of a rally, instead of going on and forcing a confrontation with the powers–that–be cost him the support of many young radicals. This was not all. King was now being challenged and publicly derided, more so

after he had failed in his drive against racial discrimination in Chicago. Critics also pointed out that King had also been futile in his battle against desegregation in public parks in Albany.

In his efforts to mobilise support, King, who was also loathed by many white Southern segregationists, went on a populist binge, seeking a prop–up from janitors, hospital workers, and pacifist intellectuals. His efforts were unproductive. To add to the misery, a perfidious sniper bullet felled him while standing on a hotel balcony in Memphis.

Since his death, King's standing has only expanded. He has also been described as Twentieth Century's equal of Abraham Lincoln. There's something common between the two great men – their belief in human rights in a nation quite divided against itself on the subject. The commonality extends further. Lincoln and King were assassinated for being a part of what they thought was right and just. Following his demise, Coretta, who King married in 1953, has followed her husband's footsteps as a civil rights leader. So also have King's children who have done his memory proud.

King died a martyr. Yet, in the face of the buckshot that took his life, his deep faith and belief that truth and justice would one day triumph, remained firm and unshakeable. His quest for peace is manifest in his own words: 'Have we not come to such an impasse in the modern world that we must love our enemies, or else. The chain reaction of evil, hate begetting hate, wars producing more wars, must be broken, or else we shall be plunged into the dark abyss of annihilation.'

His words still ring true today. It will do so for tomorrow, unless we change our mind–set and live like brothers whatever the colour of our skin and or faith.

Dalai Lama

1935 –

Exiled leader of peace

His Holiness, the 14th and current Dalai Lama, the fourth son of a poor peasant family, was born in Tibet, soon after the 13th Dalai Lama died. He is the spiritual leader of the Tibet Buddhists, and Head of State and sole political ruler of Tibet. He has lived in exile, in India, from the time China occupied Tibet (1960).

He hails from the Gelug sect of Tibetan Buddhism. His early education as a Buddhist monk began when he was six. After nearly twenty years of concentrated study, Dalai Lama graduated with the equivalent of a Ph.D., in Buddhist metaphysics. His degree was presented only after a rigorous twelve–week viva voce examination.

Prior to this, the Dalai Lama had to undergo pilot examinations at three celebrated monastic universities – Drepung, Sera and Ganden. The final examination was held at the Jokhang Temple in Lhasa (1959). His scholarship was intensely scrutinised by several scholars of logic. He had to undergo a debate in Buddhist philosophy with other scholars, following which he was evaluated for his understanding of the principles of monastic regulation and metaphysics. He passed with distinction and attained the highest academic degree, the Geshe Lharampa.

Dalai means 'Ocean' in Mongolian; 'Lama' means 'Spiritual teacher' in Tibetan. First bestowed as a title by the great Mongolian ruler Altan Khan upon the 3rd Dalai Lama, the exalted designation is given today to every incarnation in the lineage. The Dalai Lamas are believed to be successive appearances of Avalokiteshvara, the Bodhisattva of Compassion. However, the present Dalai Lama does not seem to endorse the view or his Buddhahood.

A Dalai Lama is not appointed or elected. He is, in a manner, born to the position. A re–embodiment of the previous one, the Dalai Lamas are thought to return to the world to serve humanity. It is also believed that when each Dalai Lama dies, he leaves behind symbols to signify his anticipated birth.

When a Dalai Lama passes into a new age, a search for the Lama's reincarnation, or tulku, usually a small child, is conducted. The emblematic representations of the previous Dalai Lama often clinch the issue of reincarnation. The future Dalai Lama is brought to a monastery for orientation. The legacy is not necessarily peaceful. It may also sometimes take the shape of a political struggle for power.

The 14th Dalai Lama is no exception. Search parties found him to be the successor of the 13th Dalai Lama, evidenced by certain ciphers and auguries.

▶ Exiled leader of peace

Previous page: The Dalai Lama has set up schools, including English, Hindi and western–style education, along with Tibetan language and culture, with the help of the Indian government. Opposite: At age 16, the Dalai Lama assumed full political power as Head of State at a time when Tibet was threatened by Chinese hegemonistic intentions.

Following a series of examinations, he was named the 14th incarnation of the Dalai Lama. The Dalai Lama, also called Gyawa Rinpoche, is revered by Tibetans as the great protector. He is also called Yeshe Norbu – the joy-fulfilling jewel.

It is common knowledge that the People's Republic of China, despite its committed resolve for religious intolerance, has declared its power to approve the naming of such reincarnations in Tibet. In the process, it has sought to apply its power on the induction of the Panchen Lama, the second–most powerful leader after Dalai Lama, who is also authorised to recognise the new Dalai Lama. It is believed that the Chinese move has been so designed as to bring in more than an element of division in Tibetan politics and governance.

The current Dalai Lama fled Tibet, but his early initiation as Dalai Lama was not without drama. The Chinese had control of his province. It is also a matter of record that the local leader demanded a huge payoff before the lad could be released. Following prolonged negotiations, the young Dalai Lama and his followers were allowed to leave the province and travel to Lhasa, the capital, where he was legitimately sworn–in as the Dalai Lama.

At age 16, the Dalai Lama assumed full political power as Head of State at a time when Tibet was threatened by Chinese hegemonistic intentions.

Four years later, the Dalai Lama went to the Chinese capital to speak to Mao Tse Tung. However, when the Chinese army invaded Tibet, the Dalai Lama and his followers had no other choice but flee to neighbouring India. Since then a government–in–exile has been run from Dharmasala, or 'Little Lhasa.' It is a government that is committed to work for the freedom of Tibet and the welfare of Tibetan refugees. The Dalai Lama has set up schools, including English, Hindi and western–style education, along with Tibetan language and culture, with the help of the Indian government. He has also encouraged Tibetan culture to flourish along with traditional handicraft which is a pride of Tibet.

The Dalai Lama has also presented his case to many world leaders and met a host of Presidents, Prime Ministers, and other leaders (including the U.N.), and the late Pope Paul VI and Pope John Paul II. On his meeting with the latter, the Dalai Lama said: 'We live in a period of great crisis, a period of troubling world developments. It is not possible to find peace in the soul without security and harmony between people. For this reason, I look forward with faith and hope to my meeting with the Holy Father; to an exchange of ideas and feelings, and to his suggestions, so as to open the door to a progressive pacification between people.' This was something that none of the previous Dalai Lamas had done – establish contact with the West. The cause of Tibet is now gaining ground worldwide though China remains inflexible in its 'Hold' on the country.

Says the Dalai Lama: 'I always believe that it is much better to have a variety of religions, a variety of philosophies, rather than one single religion or philosophy. This is necessary because of the different mental dispositions of each human being. Each religion has certain unique ideas or techniques, and learning about them can only enrich one's own faith.'

The Dalai Lama, the very embodiment of peace, philosophy, spirituality and piety, was awarded the Nobel Peace Prize in 1989. He characterises infinite compassion. He is a spiritual leader with no boundaries.

Richard Branson

1950 –

21st century titan

Sir Richard Branson KBE is a famed British entrepreneur, and is best known for his widely successful Virgin brand, a banner that encompasses a variety of business organisations.

Branson first achieved notoriety with Virgin Records, a record label that started out with multi–instrumentalist Mike Oldfield and introduced bands like the Sex Pistols and Culture Club to the world music scene.

The first album of Virgin Records went on to sell more than five million copies. At the age of 27, Branson signed The Sex Pistols to the Virgin Records label after the group was turned down by every label in Great Britain.

Over the years, he signed many superstar names including Steve Winwood, Paula Abdul, Belinda Carlisle, Genesis, Phil Collins, Peter Gabriel, Simple Minds, The Human League, Bryan Ferry, Culture Club, Janet Jackson, and The Rolling Stones. As is evident, Branson managed to turn the Virgin Music Group into a giant success.

In 1992, the Virgin Music Group including record labels, music publishing and recording studios, was sold to Thorn EMI in a $1 billion U.S. deal.

The interests of Virgin Group have since expanded into international 'Megastore' music retailing, books and software publishing, film and video editing facilities, and clubs and hotels throughout 100 companies in 15 countries.

Known for his wacky exploits used to promote his businesses, Branson is keen on playful antagonisms, exemplified by his 'Mine is bigger than yours' decals on the new Airbus A340–600 jets used by his airline. He has also made several unsuccessful attempts to fly in a hot air balloon around the world.

The hot air balloon, called the 'Virgin Atlantic Flyer,' was the first hot air balloon ever to cross the Atlantic Ocean, and was the largest ever flown reaching speeds in excess of 130 mph (209 km/h).

In 1991, Branson crossed the Pacific Ocean from Japan to Arctic Canada, a distance of 4,767 miles (7,672 km), but their track took them a claimed 10,885 km. This again broke all existing records with speeds of up to 245 mph in a balloon measuring 2.6 million cubic feet.

He formed Virgin Atlantic Airways in 1984, launched Virgin Mobile in 1999, and later failed in a 2000 bid to handle the National Lottery. He has also started a European short–haul airline, Virgin Express.

In October 2003, he teamed up with balloonist Steve Fossett as lead sponsor for an attempt to break the record for a non–stop flight around the world. A new aircraft, the GlobalFlyer, was built specially for the attempt by Scaled Composites and on March 3, 2005, at about 01:50 PM CST, Fossett completed the record–breaking flight after 67 hours and 1 minute, with an average speed of nearly 300 mph.

On September 25, 2004 he announced the signing of a deal under which a new space tourism company, Virgin Galactic, will license the technology behind SpaceShipOne to take paying passengers into suborbital space. The group plans to make flights available to the public by late 2007 with tickets priced at $190,000.

Branson has been tagged as a 'Transformational leader' by management lexicon, with his maverick strategies and his stress on the Virgin Group as an organisation driven on informality and information, one that's bottom heavy rather than strangled by top–level management.

Walt Disney

1901 – 1966

Animation pioneer

Walt Disney, the genius of 'animagination,' was born in Chicago. Named after his father and his close chum Walter Parr, a preacher, Disney had his formal education at Benton Grammar School. He graduated in 1917. He enlisted as a volunteer ambulance driver in World War I, by changing his year of birth to 1900 and served in France.

After the war, Disney returned home and began looking for a job. He toyed with the idea of becoming a political cartoonist. Instead, he took up a job in Posman–Rubin Commercial Art Studio. It was here that he came in contact with Ub Iwerks. In 1920, the duo got together and created Iwerks–Disney Commercial Artists.

Two years later, Disney began making shorts based on fairy–tales. He also began experimenting with live–action and animation. His shorts were well–received, although he felt they were not financially viable. He decided that it was time he worked on a combination map, which included both live–action and animation in unison. Following his initial forays in the form, Disney created 'Alice's Wonderland.' There was a young actress Virginia Davis who played Alice. However, Disney soon ran short of funds and his company became insolvent.

Disney finally found distributors in Hollywood and signed a contract with them, but he was now confronted with a major drawback. He had no studio; he did not have artists or actors. Before long, with the support of his older brother, Roy Oliver, Disney formed a small studio, from which they made ten successful films.

The Disney brothers now bought a bigger studio, and created a cast of their own animated stars. In 1925, Walt changed the name of his company from The Disney Brothers Studio to The Walt Disney Studio and became the head of the studio; he was just 25. He grew a moustache to look older than his age, because he felt that not many would take him seriously.

In 1927, the Alice series came to an abrupt end, because the distributors felt its appeal was declining. Disney now developed a new animated series, starring a rabbit who he called 'Oswald, the Lucky Rabbit.' The rabbit looked old, and a bit out of place. Disney performed cosmetic surgery making it a slimmer, better–looking Oswald. It was an instant success.

While musical scores added a new dimension to his shorts, Disney's 'The Three Little Pigs,' for instance, was so successful that it created a novel record in cartoon films. The title song, composed by Frank Churchill, was as big a hit as any of the most popular numbers today.

Disney made his first feature–length film 'Snow White and the Seven Dwarfs,' in 1937 – the maiden American animated feature in colour. This was followed by 'Fantasia' and 'Pinocchio' (1940).

Following World War II, Disney was faced with hard times. In 1949, Disney, with his family, moved to a new home in Los Angeles. It was here that he first laid his plans, with the help of friends, to work on his own miniature Carolwood Pacific Railroad in his backyard. This was Walt's first walk into his dream project – Disneyland.

He opened Disneyland, a theme park, in 1955. It was an instantaneous success. Disneyland is today an extraordinary amusement park – a magnificent dreamland like no other in the world. One cannot imagine a world without Walt Disney who transformed the entertainment industry into what we know today.

Bill Gates

1955 –

The world's most influential individual

Born in Seattle, Washington, to a corporate lawyer, and Mary Maxwell Gates, a school teacher, Bill Gates completed his early education at one of his home–town exclusive schools, Lakeside. It was here that he first developed programming skills on the minicomputer. He later enrolled at Harvard University, and dropped out. It was a blessing in disguise as he went head–on into his passion – software development.

By the age of 17, Gates had sold his first programme – a timetabling system for his school, which earned him $4,200. In the mid–1970s, Gates co–authored with his friend, Paul Allen, the original Altair BASIC interpreter for the Altair 8800 (the first commercially successful personal computer). His exemplar was enthused by BASIC, an easy–to–learn programming language.

Now worth a whopping $46.6 billion, and ranked #1 richest man in the world, Gates is said to be an agnostic, but he firmly believes in human welfare. He has committed a great deal of wealth for the uplift of the poorest of the poor and HIV research. He has helped presidents like George Bush, with campaign funds, to win the elections (2004). 1975 was Gates', annus mirabilis. He and Allen co–founded Microsoft Corporation to market their version of BASIC, called Microsoft BASIC. It was the fundamental interpreted computer language of the MS–DOS operating system – and, the torch that first lit Microsofts opening commercial success.

The following year, Gates shocked the computer community by saying that a commercial market existed for computer software. He also asserted that computer software should not be copied without the publisher's permission. If anyone copied, he said, it was tantamount to piracy. Gates was on solid ground, but his proposal was quite a stunning element in an era where ham radio and hacker morality and innovative knowledge were liberally shared in the community.

Gates was spot on about the market projection. His brilliant efforts paid off. Soon, Microsoft Corporation became a world leader, and one of the world's most successful commercial enterprises. That it went on to become a lead player in the creation of a retail software industry is common knowledge. When IBM was planning to enter the personal computer market with its IBM Personal Computer (1981), Gates licensed MS–DOS, which it had acquired from a local computer manufacturer to IBM. How this happened is part of computer industry folklore – that Gates capitalised on an IBM gaffe laid the

▶ # The world's most influential individual

Previous page: Bills Gates could claim to be the most influential individual in the Twentieth Century
Opposite: Notwithstanding his enormous wealth and hard-nosed command of the global computer industry, Gates continues to live with his eternal obsession – programming.

foundation for his company's astounding success. Some even accused Gates of unethical leanings. However, what he did was astounding. He marketed MS–DOS assertively to manufacturers of IBM–PC replicas. This led to unparalleled recognition for Microsoft on par with IBM.

Gates quickly used Microsoft's expanding wherewithal to put out of place competitors such as WordPerfect, and Lotus 1-2-3. While it is whispered that Gates planted Microsoft programmers to include a unique cipher in one of the MS–DOS versions to make Lotus 1-2-3 produce errors, this remains an allegation that has never been proved.

And, by the latter part of the 1980s, Gates joined hands with IBM. In a dramatic development, in May 1991, Gates announced to Microsoft employees that the OS/2 partnership with IBM was history and Microsoft would focus its platform efforts on Windows and the NT core. The rest is contemporary history – as Gates and Windows opened the doors of the entire world, IBM OS/2 went into oblivion.

Gates scored yet another major victory with his free–packaged Internet Explorer. Ever the dreamer, Gates, with his amazing business acumen, also became animated about the possibilities of compact disc for storage – CD–ROM. It is now a huge reality.

Gates established Microsoft's niche and widened the company's range of products – most importantly, he sustained its magnificent growth. Not that whatever he has engineered for the company, has been fair. There have been cases where his operative procedures have been ruled as unlawful. When Gates promoted his long–time friend and Microsoft executive Steve Ballmer to the role of Chief Executive Officer, he began to don the role of Chief Software Architect, a perfect insignia for a man who laid

the Chip of Good Hope, and revolutionised computer technology on a global scale like never before.

In 1994, Gates married Melinda French. The couple have three children and live in a mammoth, Nineteenth Century manor, converted into an ultra–modern earth–sheltered home overlooking Lake Washington. Needless to say, the mansion is fitted with advanced electronic systems. It has a large domed reading room which is the private library.

The Bill & Melinda Gates Foundation, a charitable organisation, is one major humanistic project that Gates has founded. As critics reckon that it is just a masquerade to cover for the wealth he has amassed, not to speak of Microsoft's monopolistic hegemony, it is a matter of fact that the Foundation has provided grants and funds for minority college scholarships, AIDS preclusion, diseases of the developing world, and other causes. It is also reported that the Foundation currently provides almost ninety per cent of the world's budget for the endeavour to eradicate poliomyelitis. When Gates and Melinda donated US$5 billion to their Foundation, in 1999, it was recorded as the largest single donation ever made by living individuals. Besides this, Gates has donated more than $100 million to help children suffering from AIDS, yet another noteworthy contribution.

Notwithstanding his enormous wealth and hard–nosed command of the global computer industry, Gates continues to live with his eternal obsession of programming. He is known just as much for his aggressive business strategy and belligerent style of management.

Bills Gates could claim to be the most influential individual of the Twentieth Century.

Elvis Presley

1935 – 1977

The king of rock

Elvis Aaron Presley was an American singer who had an effect on world culture rivalled only by The Beatles and Chuck Berry. He started his career under the name The Hillbilly Cat and was soon nicknamed Elvis the Pelvis because of his sexually suggestive performance style. In terms of sheer record sales, Elvis' impact is utterly phenomenal and eclipses any other recording artist

Presley was born in a one–room house in Tupelo, Mississippi, to Vernon Elvis Presley and Gladys Love Smith Presley. He was raised both in Tupelo and later in Memphis, Tennessee, where his family moved when he was 13. He had a twin brother (Jesse Garon Presley) who died at birth. They would move to Lauderdale Courts public housing development in 1949. It was here where Elvis would be near Memphis music and cultural influences like Beale Street, Ellis Auditorium, Poplar Tunes record store with Sun Studio about a mile away. The young Elvis took up guitar at 11 and would practice in the basement laundry room at Lauderdale Courts. He would play gigs in the malls and courtyards of the Courts with other musicians that lived there.

In the summer of 1953 he paid $4 to record the first of two double–sided demo acetates at Sun Studios. The demo consisted of 'My Happiness' and 'That's When Your Heartaches Begin,' popular ballads of the time. While Presley claimed to have recorded the demo as a birthday present for his mother, this is probably untrue, since Gladys Presley's birthday was in April and he recorded the acetate in July. Sun Records founder Sam Phillips and assistant Marion Keisker heard the discs and, recognising Presley's nascent talent, called him in June 1954 to fill in for a missing ballad singer. Although the session did not prove fruitful, Sam put Elvis together with local musicians Scotty Moore and Bill Black to see what might develop. During a rehearsal break on July 5, 1954, Elvis started fooling around with a blues song written by Arthur Crudup called 'That's All Right'. Philips liked the record and released it as a single backed with Elvis' hopped–up version of Bill Monroe's bluegrass song 'Blue Moon Of Kentucky.' The record was a huge local hit in Memphis after WHBQ aired it two days later, and regular touring started to expand his fame beyond Tennessee.

Elvis toured incessantly throughout the south and southwest, also appearing 50 times on the regional show Louisiana Hayride (his first appearance was on March 3, 1955). Hayride founder and producer Horace Logan had shrewdly signed Elvis to weekly appearances after noting

The king of rock

Previous page: Presley engineered the rock–and–roll boom the world over.
Opposite:Presley starred in 33 films, and made history with his TV appearances, and specials.

the audience reaction to the then–unknown singer. It was during Elvis' last appearance on the Hayride that Logan announced, 'Elvis has left the building', desperate to quell the screaming teenagers trying to reach Elvis as he exited the stage. The phrase has been popularised and is commonly used in joking reference to many, often unimportant, events being over as if they were as popular as an Elvis concert.

On August 18, 1955 his parents signed a contract with Colonel Parker, thereby ending the relationship with Sun Studio. Elvis signed with RCA Records on November 21, 1955. On January 27, 1956 the single 'Heartbreak Hotel' / 'I Was the One' was released. It was the sixth single of his career. Unlike the previous singles, this one did chart, reaching #1 in April 1956.

Over the next twenty–one years, until his death in 1977, Elvis had 146 Hot 100 hits, 112 top 40 hits, 72 top 20 hits and 40 top 10 hits; all of these are the most anyone has yet achieved. 'Don't Be Cruel' and 'Hound Dog' topped the pop, black and country charts in 1956. A string of hit records followed as the public's desire for his product seemed insatiable.

The 1960s saw the quality of Presley's recorded output drop, although he was still capable of creating records equal to his best and did so on the infrequent occasions where he was presented with decent material at his movie recording sessions. In 1960 the album Elvis is Back was recorded.

This, like his first two albums, Elvis Presley and Elvis, are considered by many of his fans to be his best work. With this drop–off, and in the face of the social upheaval of the 1960s and the British Invasion spearheaded by The Beatles, Presley's star faded slightly before a triumphant TV comeback special on NBC (aired on December 3, 1968) that saw him return to his rock and roll roots. His 1969 return to live performances, first in Las Vegas and then across the country, was noted for the constant stream of sold–out shows, with many setting attendance records in

the venues where he performed.

His most successful concert was the Elvis Aloha Concert in Hawaii, which was broadcast worldwide via satellite in January 1973. It was a milestone for Presley's career and his biggest audience to date.

Beginning with Love Me Tender, Presley starred in 31 motion pictures, having signed to multiple long–term contracts on the advice of his manager. These were usually musicals based around Presley performances, and marked the beginning of his transition from rebellious rock and roller to all–round family entertainer. Elvis was praised by all his directors, including the highly respected Michael Curtiz, as unfailingly polite and extremely hardworking.

The movies Jailhouse Rock (1957), King Creole (1958), and Flaming Star (1960) are widely regarded as his best among film critics. Among fans, Blue Hawaii (1961) and Viva Las Vegas (1964) are highly praised. Between 1956 and 1969, Presley starred in 31 films.

On May 1, 1967 Elvis married Priscilla Anne Beaulieu at the Aladdin Hotel in Las Vegas. Priscilla had been the step–daughter of Presley's commanding officer in Germany during his Army stint. Incredibly, Elvis managed to talk Priscilla's mother and step–father into allowing the underaged girl to live with him at Graceland. Daughter, Lisa Marie, was born on February 1, 1968. After their divorce in 1973, Lisa lived with Priscilla.

He died at his home Graceland in Memphis, Tennessee on August 16, 1977. He was found on the floor of his bedroom's bathroom ensuite by girlfriend Ginger Alden who had been asleep in his bed. He was transported to Baptist Memorial Hospital where doctors pronounced him dead at 3.30pm. He was only 42 years old. Now, more than 30 years after his death, Presley remains the foremost pop icon of the Twentieth Century. His image, especially his trademark forelock, is instantly recognisable. He is still the gold standard against which modern notions of fame are measured.

Frank Sinatra

1915 – 1998

Finest vocalist of all time

Francis Albert Sinatra was an American singer who is considered one of the finest vocalists of all time, renowned for his impeccable phrasing and timing. At age 37, Sinatra launched a second career as a film actor, and became admired for a screen persona distinctly tougher than his smooth singing style.

Born in Hoboken, New Jersey as the son of a quiet father and a talented, tempestuous mother, Sinatra decided to become a singer after hearing Bing Crosby on the radio. He began singing in small clubs in New Jersey and eventually attracted the attention of band–leader Harry James.

After a brief stint with James, he joined the Tommy Dorsey Orchestra in 1940 where he rose to fame as a singer. His vast appeal to the 'bobby soxers', as teenage girls were then called, revealed a whole new audience for popular music, which had appealed mainly to adults up to that time. He was the first singing teen idol.

He later signed with Columbia Records as a solo artist with some success, particularly during the musicians' recording strikes. Vocalists were not part of the musician union and were allowed to record during the ban by using a capella vocal backing.

Sinatra's singing career was in decline in the late 1940s and early 1950s when he made a spectacular comeback as an actor in From Here to Eternity (1953), which won him a Best Supporting Actor Academy Award. He later appeared in many films, the most noteworthy being The Man with the Golden Arm, and The Manchurian Candidate. In 1954, Sinatra played a crazed, coldblooded assassin determined to kill the President in the thriller Suddenly also starring Sterling Hayden. Critics have found Sinatra's performance one of the most chilling portrayals of a psychopath ever committed to film. Sinatra, however, insisted the film be removed from distribution after he learned that Lee Harvey Oswald had watched it shortly before he assassinated President Kennedy.

Soon after his film debut, Sinatra's singing career rebounded. During the 1950s, he signed with Capitol Records, where he worked with many of the finest arrangers of the era, most notably Nelson Riddle and Billy May, and with whom he made a series of highly regarded recordings. By the early 1960s, he was a big enough star to start his own record label: Reprise Records. His position with the label earned him the long–lasting nickname 'The Chairman of the Board'.

In the 1950s and 1960s, Sinatra was a popular attraction in Las Vegas. He was friends with many other entertainers, including Dean Martin and Sammy Davis, Jr. Together, along with actor Peter Lawford and comedian Joey Bishop, they formed the core of the Rat Pack, a loose group of entertainers who were friends and socialised together.

Sinatra played a major role in the desegregation of Nevada hotels and casinos in the 1960s. Sinatra led his fellow members of the Rat Pack in refusing to patronise hotels and casinos that denied service to Sammy Davis Jr., an African–American. As the Rat Pack became the subject of great media attention due to the release of the film Ocean's Eleven, many hotels and casinos, desiring the attention that would come from the presence of Sinatra and the Rat Pack in their properties, relented on their policies of segregation.

Sinatra died in 1998 of a heart attack in Los Angeles, following a long illness from coronary heart disease, kidney disease, bladder cancer and senility.

Steven Spielberg

1946 –

Movie mastermind

Steven Allan Spielberg, KBE, is craftsman of enormous repute who has made many great movies from science fiction and the sublime to historical and patriotic subjects. In the midst of it all, he has invited and incited controversial themes. Hugely successful at the box–office he is today labelled a movie mogul.

Spielberg went to Long Beach University where he dropped out to pursue a career in the entertainment industry. He first worked as an assistant editor in the classic Western 'Wagon Train' (1957). He also directed short–films, in his formative years, 'Battle Squad,' 'Escape to Nowhere' and 'The Last Gun.' Spielberg directed a brace of movies that prophesied his own future in tinsel town.

From his early days, Spielberg had a flair for art. He actually grew up making films. He made his first short–film at age 18. Spielberg's first directorial effort was a part in Rod Serling's 'Night Gallery.' He made a major impact with the 1971 TV 'Movie–of–the–Week' called 'Duel,' which was later released in theatres. A cult classic, the movie captures a truck driver furtively petrifying a common city–dweller.

Spielberg debuted into theatrical films with 'The Sugarland Express,' a story about a husband and wife attempting to escape the law. This won him significant acclaim. Thereafter, he expanded his horizons in Hollywood with horror–adventure–based films such as 'Jaws' which won four Academy Awards and collected over a record $100 million at the box–office.

From his youthful days, Spielberg was fascinated by UFOs. When Alexander Salkind asked him to direct 'Superman,' Spielberg instead decided to make 'Close Encounters of the Third Kind' (1977), a magnificent film of its kind, and one of the best in the genre till date. With his grasp of both the mainstream and commercial web, Spielberg had now become hugely successful though the film brought him some derision from critics.

Spielberg's greatest film work which he made with his friend George Lucas, 'Raiders of the Lost Ark,' is now part of movie folklore. This led to two sequels, both directed by Spielberg and produced by Lucas. In 1982, Spielberg ventured into his alien obsession again and made 'ET, the Extra–Terrestrial.' Needless to say, the film was a box-office success.

As it so often happens with geniuses, Spielberg has not been given the tag of a great movie–maker in the league of what makes directors of films such as 'Godfather' truly great. Spielberg had to wait for real critical acclaim to come his way. This emerged when he made 'Schindler's List,' a movie based on a novel about a man who forfeited everything to save thousands of people during the Holocaust years. The film earned Spielberg the regular Academy Award for Best Director. It also won the Best Picture award.

When Spielberg began filming the project, 'Ai: Artificial Intelligence,' a futuristic story of a human android pining for love, in 2001, the movie had everything and more a blockbuster ought to need and be. Unfortunately, the film faired poorly at the box–office. It was a personal blow to Spielberg's reputation. Spielberg recently, re–emerged with his brilliance with 'Minority Report,' starring Tom Cruise as an innovative cop who's on the run from his own future, not to speak of 'Catch Me if you Can,' a tale about a con–man, featuring Leonardo di Caprio and Tom Hanks. Spielberg's 'The Terminal,' featuring Hanks, was another success story. Spielberg has, so far, won two Academy Awards for Best Director – 'Schindler's List' and 'Saving Private Ryan.'

The Beatles

1962 – 1970

The greatest musical influence of our time

The Beatles were the most influential and successful popular music group of the rock era. Few artists of any sort, in any era, have achieved The Beatles' combination of popular success, critical acclaim and broad cultural influence.

The Beatles were John Lennon (rhythm guitar/keyboards), Paul McCartney (bass/piano/guitars), George Harrison (lead guitar/sitar), and Ringo Starr (drums), all from Liverpool, Merseyside, in England. Although Lennon and McCartney were initially the principal songwriters, Harrison and Starr made significant contributions as the band matured. George Martin produced almost all of the Beatles' recordings.

The Beatles created a sensation in late 1963 in the U.K. (the phenomenon was dubbed 'Beatlemania' by the British press), notable for the hordes of screaming and swooning young women the group inspired. Beatlemania went to North America in early 1964, and the band's popularity extended across much of the world. Within the space of five years, their music progressed from the apparent simplicity of their early hits (such as 'She Loves You' and 'I Want to Hold Your Hand') to artistically ambitious suites of songs (such as the albums Revolver, Sgt. Pepper's Lonely Hearts Club Band and Abbey Road). By writing their own songs,

exploring the possibilities of the recording studio and striving for unprecedented quality in every recording they released, the Beatles had far reaching effects on popular music. The band made feature films that were the subject of unprecedented press scrutiny, and became symbolic leaders of the international youth counterculture of the 1960s, publicly exploring Eastern mysticism, psychedelic drugs and revolutionary politics. The group disbanded in 1970.

Beatle mania began in Britain on 13 October 1963 with a televised appearance at the London Palladium, then exploded in the U.S. following three appearances of the Beatles on The Ed Sullivan Show on 9 February, 16 February and 23 February 1964. The pop–music band became a worldwide phenomenon with worshipful fans and angry denunciations by cultural commentators and established performers such as Frank Sinatra, sometimes on grounds of the music (which was thought crude and unmusical) or their appearance (their hair was scandalously long).

In 1964 they held the top five places on Billboard's Hot 100, a feat that has never been repeated.

In 1965 they were instated as Members of the Order of the British Empire. Lennon and Harrison began experimenting with LSD in that year and McCartney would do the same near the end of 1966. Lennon caused a backlash against The

► # The greatest musical influence of our time

Previous page: Though the Fab Four were originally famous for light pop music, their later work achieved a mix of critical and literary acclaim that nobody has been able to match. Opposite: They are the best–selling musical group of all time.

Beatles the following year when in an interview he claimed that Christianity was dying and he quipped that the Beatles were 'more popular than Jesus.' Eventually he apologised at a press conference, acquiescing to objections by many religious groups, including the Holy See, having Beatles' records banned or burned across the American South and receiving threats from groups such as the Ku Klux Klan.

The Beatles performed their last concert before paying fans in Candlestick Park in San Francisco on 29 August 1966. From this time until the group dissolved in early 1970 The Beatles concentrated on making some of the most remarkable recorded music of the Twentieth Century. The group's compositions and musical experiments raised their artistic reputations while they retained their tremendous popularity. The Beatles' financial fortunes took a turn for the worse, however, when their manager, Brian Epstein, died in 1967 and the band's affairs began to unravel. The members began to drift apart. Their final live performance was on the roof at the Apple studios in London in January 1969 during the 'Get Back' sessions and was featured both on the 'Let It Be' album and the 'Let It Be' film. In 1969 , largely due to McCartney's efforts, they recorded their final album, Abbey Road. The band officially broke up in 1970, and any hopes of a reunion were crushed when Lennon was assassinated in 1980.

However, a virtual reunion occurred in 1995 with the release of two original Lennon recordings which had the additional contributions of the remaining Beatles mixed in to create two hit singles: 'Free as a Bird' and 'Real Love'. Three albums of unreleased material and studio outtakes were also released, as well as a documentary and television miniseries, in a project known as 'The Beatles Anthology'. Unlike their contemporaries the Rolling Stones, blues seldom directly influenced the Beatles. Though they drew inspiration from an eclectic variety of sources, their home idiom was closer to pop music. Their distinctive vocal harmonies were influenced by early Motown artists in the U.S. Chuck Berry was perhaps the most fundamental progenitor of the Beatles' sound; the Beatles covered 'Roll Over Beethoven' and 'Rock And Roll Music' early in their careers on record (with most other Berry classics heard in their live repertoire). Chuck Berry's influence is also heard, in an altered form, in later songs such as 'Everybody's Got Something to Hide Except Me And My Monkey' (1968) and 'Come Together' (1969) (when 'Come Together' was released, the owner of Chuck Berry's copyrights sued John Lennon for copyright infringement of his song 'You Can't Catch Me', after which the two reached an amicable settlement, the terms of which included the agreement that Lennon cover some Chuck Berry songs as a solo artist).

Some people claim The Beatles' biggest influence was Elvis Presley. This is a matter of debate. But others claim that, given that The Beatles sound little or nothing like Elvis, and little of his handprint can be seen in their catalogue, and also given that they have so many other influences in chamber pop, R&B, soul, and early rock, Paul and John must have obviously gotten that feeling from a lot of other artists, and Paul would have surely picked up a guitar due to that feeling he got from any of the myriad other influences.

To many, the group's musical appeal lay in the contrasting styles of John and Paul. Too much of John's music might seem sarcastic, self–absorbed and schizophrenic, and a whole album of Paul could possibly be perceived as a little too safe, perhaps even bordering on saccharine. Indeed, after the group dissolved and the former partners put forth solo releases, critical complaints about their albums often centered on precisely those excesses. This was a phenomenon that has cast a huge shadow over generations and a time when music would be changed forever.

Andy Warhol

1930 – 1987

Influential New Age artist

A ndy Warhol was the ultimate name in marrying art and the forces that swept the twentieth century decisively media, popular culture and stardom. A quintessential American who managed to match the popularity of Norman Rockwell at home and Salvador Dali abroad, Warhol imparted aesthetic seriousness to seemingly banal and cheap images. His mass following as an artist and filmmaker derived from a freakish ability to convert vaudeville silliness into vintage weightiness.

Warhol's 'Pop Art' was the most depressing and vivid representation of American consumerism and material progress. Purists frowned and critics were insulted, but Warhol made the press with unending regularity and remained in public consciousness far longer than any of his contemporaries. Showbiz and glamour were his natural arenas, the atelier being only a launch pad for his flamboyance.

Born as Andrew Warhola in Pennsylvania State to Czech migrants who laboured in coalmines, Warhol was a loner at school. He suffered three nervous breakdowns between the ages of eight and 10 and utilised recovery periods for imitating advertisement drawings. Eccentricity, Warhol's second nature, had clear origins in childhood. He would produce art while being mentally disturbed. His mother fostered the typical love immigrants had for all things American and gave him a Hershey Bar every time he finished a page in his colouring book.

Warhol glided through uneventful college years in Pittsburgh hoping to become an art teacher in public schools. He worked in departmental stores pouring over fashion magazines. Warhol's trademark sense of style and love for commercialism were developed by 1949, when he began illustrating women's shoes and other accessories for lifestyle articles in New York. An art director's dream, Warhol adapted to any subject, be it crime, haute couture or corporate image building. In the decade of the 1950s, he put an astounding amount of energy and refinement into work of the most perishable nature.

Warhol was unorthodox to the core. Unlike aspiring artists who dressed in formal suit and tie, he was 'Raggedy Andy' wearing sneakers, chino pants and open necked shirts. His portfolio was a crumpled bag graced by cockroaches. His quirky signature did not capitalise the 'A' in Andy. Determined to carve out a place in history, Warhol leapfrogged from illustrations to the fine art of painting in the 1960s. His series on comic–strip characters like Superman, Popeye and Dick Tracy found few buyers

▶ Influential New Age artist

Previous page: Warhol imparted aesthetic seriousness to seemingly banal and cheap images.
Opposite: Though Warhol painted sensitive and repulsive works depicting shootings, racial violence and nuclear war, Hollywood was fascinated by this arch populist.

in New York galleries. He was accused of trivialising a sublime medium. Before and After (1962) was a simple reflection of the 'nose job' rage that had taken the beauty industry by storm. Warhol's Dollar Bill and Soup Can paintings won sudden acceptance and fame. Marilyn Monroe, Elizabeth Taylor and Elvis Presley, considered vulgar and crass subjects in charmed Manhattan circles, got new leases of life from Warhol's brush. One admirer wrote, 'There is a canniness, almost a delicacy, to Warhol's crudities.' His 'Popism' provoked outrage and admiration, extreme reactions to an audacious mind.

Though Warhol painted sensitive and repulsive works depicting shootings, racial violence and nuclear war, Hollywood was fascinated by this arch populist. In 1965, he claimed to be a 'Retired artist' and took to the movies. He made numerous films like Empire, Chelsea Girls, Harlot and Poor Little Rich Girl and introduced new superstars from obscure ranks, though never really abandoning painting. Blue Movie (1969) was criticised for obscenity. Aware of his own rising status as a star in the media, he drew several self–portraits that added to notoriety. A pompadour wig buttressed his celebrity look.

In 1968, Warhol survived two slug shots from the gun of a male–hating maniac. When friends suggested that access to his studio (The Factory) should be restricted for security reasons, Warhol responded typically: 'Without the crazy, druggy people jabbering away and doing their insane things, I would lose my creativity. After all, they had been my total inspiration.' The 1970s witnessed a post–Pop Warhol, revelling in portrait wallpapers of Mao Tse Tung. His paintings of the Soviet hammer and sickle surprised observers by throwing light on alien ways of life. After a ten–year romance with western decadence, Warhol's haunting portrait of his mother in 1974 showed he could operate in poignant and glamour–free environments as well. He aroused colonialist guilt among his

American audience with The American Indian (1977) and demanded an understanding of homosexuality through Sex Parts (1978). Although the dominant impression of Warhol as a champion of reprobate American culture existed, his latter–day prints strove to confront uncomfortable aspects of American life that other artists of the period seemed to sidetrack. 'The war and the bomb worry me', he once admitted.

Warhol religiously kept a diary from 1976 to the end of his life. When the condensed version was published in book form, it became an international bestseller for party gossip and an intimate look into Warhol's enigmatic persona. He emerges from the diary as a caustic observer of the rich and the famous, leading some to the interpretation of his pop art as a social commentary on the debauched nature of American hedonism.

Warhol was self–conscious like many other American idols, noting when and where fans mobbed him or which researcher or newspaper wrote about him. One encounter where the showman artist's ego was hurt read: 'I went over to Muhammad Ali and said hi, but he looked at me blankly. He didn't seem to know who I was. So, I got embarrassed and got away.' A wealthy man who rose from poverty, Warhol diligently recorded every minor expense out of his pocket. He was a hypochondriac who feared hospitals and operations.

Warhol was the most influential New Age artist of his time in the Western hemisphere. A legion of younger painters received baptism ideas from his version of pop. He heralded the 'Return of the figure' in art, carried forward by successors who felt no guilt in sketching the paparazzi's darlings. He bequeathed novel techniques like 'Multiple' and 'Gridded' painting. A nonconformist reformer, he converted the taboo into the respectable and reminded the world that banal experiences could actually contain profound dimensions.

Harry Houdini

1874 – 1926

The master of many feats

Harry Houdini was born in Budapest, Hungary of Jewish descent. His father first migrated to the U.S. and served as rabbi of the Zion Reform Jewish Congregation. He later moved to New York City to a boarding address, and thereafter, with his entire family, to a permanent home.

Since the family was not well-off, Houdini began to work at an early age. When he happened to witness a travel magician's bundle of tricks, Houdini knew what he wanted and started practising the crafty art. He made his debut in October 1883 as a contortionist and trapeze entertainer.

He ran away from home, when he was 12, and made a living by tagging along circuses and side-shows. He reunited with his family, one year later.

When he was 15, Harry happened to read memoirs of the French Magician Jean Robert-Houdin. His name to Harry was akin to what the falling apple was to Newton. He dreamt of being the next Robert-Houdin. He added the letter 'i' to his name and became Houdini. With his new 'Identity,' Harry began to do regular shows at a salary of $12 per week. When his father passed away, Harry who was 18, took up a job as a cutter in a necktie factory.

Thereafter he did odd jobs and in a variety of trades including a courier, an electrical driller, a photographer, and an assistant to a locksmith. A fitness fanatic, Houdini had a supple physique, quite essential for a performing artist.

It was around this time that he formed a 'Double act' with his brother, Theo. This laid the foundation for their spectacular 'Substitution Trunk' or 'Metamorphosis Illusion.' It is said that this delusive act was performed by Houdini over 11,000 times during his stunning career.

In June 1894 Houdini married Wilhelmina Beatrice Rahner – another performing artiste. She soon replaced Houdini's brother. The husband–wife team now began to perform at travelling fairs, events, shows and so on. To add variety to their repertoire, Houdini also taught himself how to escape out of a strait-jacket.

Within a few years, Houdini also developed the 'Challenge' Handcuff Act. He dared anyone that could produce a pair of handcuffs from which he could not escape. The prize: $100. Not once was Houdini found wanting in his escape script. He was now the 'Handcuff King,' but his career as a legendary magician had not yet reached its great heights.

▶ The master of many feats

Previous page: Harry Houdini captivated millions with his antics which were captured each week by newsreel and and newspapers around the world. Opposite: Houdini was known for the famed 'Bridge Jump' by plummeting into San Francisco Bay, complete with a 75–pound ball and chain bound to his ankles, not to speak of handcuffs on his wrists.

He was not running out of ideas. What he needed was a prop – something that was unique. When Martin Beck, a vaudeville agent, suggested that Houdini should remain focused on his illusions and escapes, not hanker after daft conjuring, the magician in Houdini knew what it meant for his career. Beck gave Houdini the top title in his Orpheum Circuit. The catchphrase that now caught on with the public's imagination was Houdini's challenge to the police – 'Put me in any jail, with handcuffs, and I will escape.' This catapulted Beck's idea manifold – it was huge publicity. Houdini's earnings also expanded from $60.00 to $125.00 per week.

Houdini went to London in 1900. He escaped from a pair of handcuffs at England's famous Scotland Yard! Next, he jumped into the Seine River, in Paris, with handcuffs and, again, escaped. He could escape at the drop of a hat. Needless to say, he became famous and, in the process, was now the highest paid entertainer in Europe ($2,000 per week). The Houdinis soon purchased a house in New York City.

Houdini's enormous reputation grew as he mastered many more amazing feats among them were the sunken packing crates, a huge paper bag, where he did not once rip the paper while escaping, padded cells, a roll–top desk, burglar–proof safes, a preserved giant squid, a giant football, an iron boiler, a diving suit, a U.S. mail pouch and a plate glass box. To top it all, Houdini 'Escaped' from the death cell in a Washington jail. He also did the famed 'Bridge Jump' by plummeting into San Francisco Bay, complete with a 75–pound ball and chain bound to his ankles, not to speak of handcuffs on his wrists. Houdini also pioneered his famous escape from a gigantic milk can filled with water and padlocked.

There were several other escapades he performed successfully. He escaped from the mouth of a big gun before the fuse burned out; and, he escaped from a weighted packing case dropped overboard from a barge. In 1914, he built the famous 'Chinese Water Torture Cell,' where he was locked and put upside down by his feet in water. He managed to escape again! He also successfully launched his 'Walking through a Brick Wall' fantasy. He followed it up with a suspended strait–jacket escape while hanging from a rope attached to high–rise buildings. Hundreds of curious onlookers always gathered at his well publicised venues and could not believe their eyes.

Houdini also performed the 'Vanishing Elephant,' a grand illusory act, followed by another escape feat from a buried coffin. Not surprisingly, he played the hero in a series of film thrillers (1919). He also founded Martinka & Co., a magic company, and introduced the famous Needle Trick, where he swallowed needles and thread and, thereafter, expelled them from his mouth with the thread intact!

The man who lay underwater for over 90 minutes in a sealed casket to beat an existing world record, Houdini continued his 'Bashing' of charlatans and tricksters without respite exposing their tall claims, and false acts of trickery.

Yet, he himself once went too far. When asked if he could take a punch on his stomach which he did as a routine, by any man, Houdini said 'Yes.' In 1926, in what appeared to be a regular blow, delivered by one gentleman on his stomach burst his appendix. Houdini died due to resulting complications.

Harry Houdini captivated millions with his antics which were captured each week by newsreel and and newspapers around the world.

Pablo Picasso

1881 – 1973

Creative genius

No single artist in the last hundred years can plausibly challenge Pablo Ruiz Picasso's perch at the very top of the creative genius pyramid. Panegyrists have proclaimed in his honour, 'The twentieth century began and ended with Picasso.' Painter, sculptor, engraver, poet, potter and many other avatars were adorned by this maestro who lent excitement, shock and wonder to the world of art.

Born to an art teacher in Andalusia, Spain, Picasso was a child prodigy. At the age of 14, he passed a reputed art academy entrance examination in one day for which a whole month was allotted. So stunning and captivating was his early work that articles were written about his oeuvre when he was merely 16. His precocious excellence was nurtured in Barcelona, where unlike other Catalonian artists, Picasso avoided melodramatic or romantic themes. Logic, discipline and ability to put mind above senses were preludes to the extraordinary art movement he would launch in time – Cubism. Picasso visited Paris in 1901 and started painting scenes of daily life including horse races, circuses, bars and dance halls. Despite changing preferences, Picasso remained unfailingly attached to reality and mostly abstained from abstraction. The colour blue pervaded his work so much so that a few of his early years are now remembered as the 'Blue Period'. Picasso's famous sympathy for the poor and forlorn was reflected in this Period. The daily struggle of the downtrodden to keep body and soul together awakened his generous impulsive nature. Human emotions in different vicissitudes found a sublime expressionist in Picasso. One observer of Picasso at work during the Period noted the 'trance–like' state' that came over him. He seemed to enter and leave his private world almost at will.

Picasso revolutionised painting by dealing a deathblow to aesthetic principles that had been sacred cows. He devised a new geometry that overhauled techniques of line, volume and colour. 'Les Demoiselles dí Avignon' heralded a modern kind of representation, borrowing from practices of African tribal art. Though the originator of Cubism in the company of Georges Braque, Picasso was not an inveterate Cubist. He constantly engendered new forms, new materials and new methods of visual expression, continually adapting his style throughout the twentieth century. In art circles, he was the 'Ringleader of innovations.' Picasso believed that painting was visual poetry. He wrote numerous unpublished poems since 1935, toying with arrangements of words, traces, lines, loops and collages.

▶ Creative genius

Previous page: Picasso revolutionised painting by dealing a deathblow to aesthetic principles that had been sacred cows.
Opposite: Picasso was a larger–than–life figure who struck friendships amongst high and low and generated heated controversies.

He defied rules of grammar, syntax and punctuation and often drew doodles and illustrations beside the verse. The tragic events of the Spanish Civil War and World War II inspired poems of violence and pain that were equally graphic in his paintings. The greatest painter of portraits, Picasso brought human figures to life within the spatial limitations of art. The eternal look of a face, transcending the temporal and casual, found no finer exponent than him. Gory, distorted faces and limbs were Picasso's way of conveying the cruelty of Fascism. He also published surrealistic plays.

Ever embroiled in the politics of his time, Picasso's tremendous output of originality bore the stamp of contemporary events. What Picasso drew at critical junctures of Spanish and world history became important archival material for researchers. In one written statement, he said, 'What do you think an artist is? he was a political being, constantly alive to heart–rending, fiery or happy events. No painting is done to decorate apartments. It is an instrument of war for attack and defence against the enemy.'

The First World War cut short Picasso's Cubist adventure. He went to Rome and designed costumes and sets for a Russian ballet. He briefly participated in the contrary artistic idiom of classicism. Picasso returned to Cubist principles for his great mural protest against Fascism–'Guernica' (1937), considered the finest limning of the horrors of war. Picasso abhorred war. His 'Flayed Head of Sheep' (1939) and many other productions centred on the theme of death. In 1945, the revelations of the Nazi concentration camps moved him to draw 'Charnel–House', a contorted jumble of bodies of what were once lively men. 'Massacre in Korea' (1951) took war painting to new heights, wherein the firing squad decimating women and children were flesh–and–iron robots whose weapons resembled not guns but more sinister instruments. The flip side of Picasso's abomination of Franco and Hitler was admiration for Stalin. The Russian army's lead in liberating Europe and the general wave of optimistic enthusiasm among progressives were motivating factors. Picasso was awarded the Lenin Peace Prize by the U.S.S.R. Though a professed communist, he still succeeded in enchanting the West due to his intransigent individualism. Henri Matisse was the only peer painter whom Picasso esteemed and competed against. Asked about other artistic influences, he retorted, 'An artist must be very careful not to look for models. As soon as one artist takes another as a model, he is lost.'

Picasso's career as a full–fledged sculptor paralleled that of his paintings. From bronzes to iron pieces, he explored every medium of sculpture. His 'Head of a Bull' (1942) was one of the most famous assemblage sculptures, confected from the parts of an abandoned bicycle. He regularly inspected garbage cans and rubbish bins to find raw material for moulding into art. He could visualise form in every object.

Picasso was a larger–than–life figure who struck friendships amongst high and low and generated heated controversies. He served on committees to choose French war artists, helped refugee Spaniards and rallied intellectuals to support the Republican cause in Spain. He married once but had some liaisons. Some of his pronouncements belittling women enraged feminists, but such utterances were part of his vast maverick personality.

In the evening of life, his vigour to paint lessened not one bit. He lamented, 'I have less and less time and more and more to say.' His quantitative and qualitative yield surpassed known limits of feasibility. A complete artist–creator, Picasso was a demiurge. The impact of his fecundity was felt across the artistic universe from the 1940s to the 1980s and beyond.

Alfred Hitchcock

1889 - 1980

A supreme technician

Alfred Hitchcock was a British film director closely associated with the suspense genre. Influenced by expressionism in Germany, he began directing in England and worked in the U.S. from 1939. With more than fifty feature films to his credit, in a career spanning six decades, he remains one of the best known and most popular directors of all time. His innovations and vision have influenced a great number of filmmakers, producers, and actors.

Hitchcock's films draw heavily on both fear and fantasy, and are known for their droll humour. They often portray innocent people caught up in circumstances beyond their control or understanding. This often involves a transference of guilt in which the 'Innocent' character's failings are transferred to another character and magnified. Another common theme is the exploration of the compatibility of men and women; Hitchcock's films often take a cynical view of traditional romantic relationships.

Although Hitchcock was an enormous star during his lifetime, he was not usually ranked highly with his contemporaneous film critics. 'Rebecca' was the only one of his films to win the Academy Award for Best Picture, although four others were nominated. He was awarded the Irving G. Thalberg Memorial Award for lifetime achievement in 1967, but never personally received an Academy Award of Merit.

The French new wave critics, especially François Truffaut, were among the first to promote his films as having artistic merit beyond entertainment. Hitchcock was one of the first directors to whom they applied their auteur theory, which stresses the centrality of the director in the movie-making process. Indeed, through his fame, public persona, and degree of creative control, Hitchcock transformed the role of the director, which had previously been eclipsed by that of the producer.

Alfred Hitchcock was born 13 August 1899 in Leytonstone, London, the second son and youngest of the three children of William Hitchcock, a greengrocer, and his wife, Emma Jane Hitchcock (nee Whelan). His family was mostly Irish Catholic. At 14, Hitchcock lost his father and left St Ignatius' College, his school at the time, to study at the School for Engineering and Navigation. After graduating, he became a draftsman and advertising designer with a cable company. About that time, Hitchcock became intrigued by photography and started working in film in London. In 1920, he obtained a full-time job at Islington Studios under its American owners, Players-Lasky, and their British successors, Gainsborough Pictures, designing

▶ A supreme technician

Previous page: Alfred Hitchcock was the Master of Suspense. He introduced generations of movie goers to what is commonly now known as a 'thriller'. Opposite: This was the Hitchcock the world grew to know – the rotund faced and pot–bellied genius with his matchless wizardry.

the titles for silent movies. In 1925, Michael Balcon of Gainsborough Pictures gave him a chance to direct his first film, 'The Pleasure Garden.'

As a major talent in a new industry with plenty of opportunity, he rose quickly. His third film, 'The Lodger.' A Story of the London Fog was released in 1927. In it, attractive blondes are strangled and the new lodger (Ivor Novello) in the Bunting family's upstairs apartment falls under heavy suspicion. This is the first truly 'Hitchcockian' film, incorporating such themes as the 'Wrong man.'

In 1929, he began work on 'Blackmail', his tenth film. While the film was in production, the studio decided to make it one of Britain's first sound pictures. In 1933, Hitchcock was once again working for Michael Balcon at Gaumont–British Picture Corporation. His first film for the company, 'The Man Who Knew Too Much' (1934), was a success. His second, 'The 39 Steps' (1935), is considered the best film from his early period. His next major success was in 1938, 'The Lady Vanishes', a clever and fast–paced film about the search for a kindly old spy (Dame May Whitty), who disappears while on board a train in the fictional country of Vandrika (a thinly–veiled reference to Nazi Germany).

By this time, he had caught the attention of Hollywood and was invited to make films in America by David O. Selznick.

With 'Rebecca' in 1940, Hitchcock made his first American film, although it was set in England and based on a novel by English author Daphne du Maurier.

Hitchcock's work during the early 1940's was very diverse, ranging from the romantic comedy, 'Mr. & Mrs. Smith' (1941), to the dark and disturbing 'Shadow of a Doubt' (1943). 'Spellbound' explored the then very fashionable subject of psychoanalysis and featured a dream sequence which was designed by Salvador Dali. The actual dream sequence in the film was considerably cut from the original planned scene that was to run for some minutes but proved too disturbing for the finished film. 'Notorious' (1946), with Ingrid Bergman, linked her to another of his most prominently recurring stars, Cary Grant. Featuring plot of Nazis, radium and South America, 'Notorious' is considered by many critics as Hitchcock's masterpiece. Its inventive use of suspense and props briefly led to Hitchcock being under surveillance by the CIA due to his use of uranium as a plot device.

'Dial M for Murder' was adapted from the popular stage play by Frederick Knott. This was originally another experimental film, with Hitchcock using the technique of 3D cinematography. 'Rear Window', starred James Stewart. Here the wheelchair–bound Stewart observes the movements of his neighbours across the courtyard. He becomes convinced that the wife of a near neighbour has been murdered. 'To Catch a Thief', set in the French Riviera, starred Kelly and Cary Grant. In 1958, Hitchcock released 'Vertigo', a film many consider to be his masterpiece. Three more recognised classics followed: 'North by Northwest' (1959), 'Psycho' (1960), and 'The Birds' (1963). These were his last great films, after which his career slowly wound down. 'Frenzy' (1972) was Hitchcock's last major success. For the first time, Hitchcock allowed nudity and profane language, which had before been taboo, in one of his films. Failing health slowed down his output over the last two decades of his life.

His films are known for featuring Alfred Hitchcock in cameos in the film — a technique used by other directors and writers including Colin Dexter in the ITV 'Inspector Morse' series.

Hitchcock was made a Knight Commander of the British Empire on January 3, 1980 by Queen Elizabeth II just four months before his death. Hitchcock died of renal failure in Los Angeles. Alfred Hitchcock introduced generations of movie goers to what is now commonly known as a 'thriller'.

Charlie Chaplin

1889 – 1977

Comedy's First Knight

Charlie Chaplin was the most famous actor in early to mid Hollywood cinema, and later also a notable director. His principal character was 'The Tramp': a vagrant with the refined manners and dignity of a gentleman who wears a tight coat, oversized pants and shoes, a derby or bowler hat, a bamboo cane, and his signature square mustache. Chaplin was one of the most creative personalities in the silent film era; he acted in, directed, scripted, produced, and eventually scored his own films.

He was born in Walworth, London, England to Charles, Sr. and Hannah Harriette Hill, both Music Hall entertainers. His parents separated soon after his birth, leaving him in the care of his increasingly unstable mother. In 1896, she was unable to find work; Charlie and his older half–brother Sydney had to be left in the workhouse at Lambeth, moving after several weeks to Hanwell School for Orphans and Destitute Children. His father died an alcoholic when Charlie was 12, and his mother suffered a mental breakdown, and was eventually admitted to the Cane Hill Asylum near Croydon. She died in 1928.

Charlie first took to the stage when, aged 5, he performed in a Music Hall in 1894, standing in for his mother. As a child, he was confined to a bed for weeks due to a serious illness, and, at night, his mother would sit at the window and act out what was going on outside. In 1900, aged 11, his brother helped get him the role of a comic cat in the pantomime Cinderella at the London Hippodrome. In 1903 he appeared in 'Jim, A Romance of Cockayne', followed by his first regular job, as the newspaper boy Billy in 'Sherlock Holmes', a part he played into 1906. This was followed by Casey's Court Circus variety show, and, the following year, he became a clown in Fred Karno's Fun Factory slapstick comedy company. According to immigration records, he arrived in America with the Karno troupe on October 2, 1912. In the Karno Company was Arthur Stanley Jefferson, who would become known as Stan Laurel. Chaplin and Laurel wound up sharing a room in a boarding house. Chaplin's act was eventually seen by film producer Mack Sennett, who hired him for his studio, the Keystone Film Company.

While Chaplin initially had difficulty adjusting to the Keystone style of film acting, he soon adapted and flourished in the medium. This was made possible in part by Chaplin developing his signature Tramp persona, and by eventually earning directorship and creative control over his films, which enabled him to become Keystone's top star and talent.

▶Comedy's First Knight

Previous page: Chaplin explained that the 'Tramp' was many–sided, a a gentleman, a poet, a dreamer, a lonely fellow, always hopeful of romance and adventure.
Opposite: Chaplin's life was a mix of triumph and trauma. Chaplin attracted as much attention for his films as for his affairs and marriages – three of which were disasters.

In 1919 he founded the United Artists studio with Mary Pickford, Douglas Fairbanks and D. W. Griffith. Although 'Talkies' (movies with sound) became the dominant mode of moviemaking soon after they were introduced in 1927, Chaplin resisted making a talkie all through the 1930s. It is a tribute to Chaplin's versatility that he also has one film credit for choreography for the 1952 film 'Limelight', and one credit as a singer for the title music of the 1928 film 'The Circus'. The best–known of several songs he composed is 'Smile', famously covered by Nat King Cole, among others.

His first sound picture, 'The Great Dictator' (1940) was an act of defiance against Adolf Hitler and fascism, filmed and released in the U.S. one year before it abandoned its policy of isolationism to enter World War II. Chaplin played a fascist dictator clearly modelled on Hitler (also with a certain physical likeness), as well as a Jewish barber cruelly persecuted by the Nazis. Hitler who was a great fan of movies, is known to have seen the film twice (accurate records were kept of movies ordered for his personal theatre).

Although Chaplin had his major successes in the U.S., he retained his British nationality. During the era of McCarthyism, Chaplin was accused of 'Un–American activities' as a suspected communist; and J. Edgar Hoover, who had instructed the FBI to keep extensive files on him, tried to end his U.S. residency. In 1952, Chaplin left the U.S. for a trip to England; Hoover learned of it and negotiated with the INS to revoke his re–entry permit. Chaplin then decided to stay in Europe, and made his home in Vevey, Switzerland. He briefly returned to the U.S. in April 1972 to receive an Honourary Oscar.

His professional successes were repeatedly overshadowed by his notorious private life. On October 23, 1918, the 28 year old Chaplin married the 16–year–old Mildred Harris. They had one child who died in infancy; they divorced in 1920. At 35, he fell in love with 16–year–old Lita Grey during preparations for 'The Gold Rush'. They married on November 26, 1924 after she became pregnant. They had two sons. Their bitter divorce in 1926 had Chaplin paying Grey a then–record–breaking $825,000 settlement. The stress of the divorce, compounded by a tax dispute, allegedly turned his hair white. The publication of court records, which included many intimate details, led to a campaign against him. He was 47 when he secretly married the 25 year old Paulette Goddard in June 1936. After some happy years, it ended in divorce in 1942. Shortly thereafter, he met Oona O'Neill, daughter of Eugene O'Neill, and married her on June 16, 1943. He was 54; she was 17. This marriage was a long and happy one, with eight children.

On March 4, 1975, after many years of self–imposed exile from his native country, he was knighted as a Knight of the British Empire by Queen Elizabeth II. The honour was first proposed in 1956, but vetoed by the British Foreign Office on the grounds that he sympathised with the left and that it would damage British relations with the U.S., at the height of the Cold War and with planning for the ill-fated invasion of Suez underway.

Chaplin died on Christmas Day, 1977 in Vevey, Switzerland at age 88, and was interred in Corsier–Sur–Vevey Cemetery in Corsier–Sur–Vevey, Vaud. On March 1, 1978, his body was stolen in an attempt to extort money from his family. The plot failed. The robbers were captured, and the body was recovered 11 weeks later near Lake Geneva. There is a statue of Chaplin in front of the alimentarium in Vevey to commemorate the last part of his life.

In a 2005 poll to find The Comedian's Comedian, he was voted among the top 20 greatest comedy acts ever by fellow comedians and comedy insiders.

Nelson Mandela

1918 –

An incomparable icon

Nelson Rolihlahla Mandela was the legendary freedom fighter who spearheaded South Africa's struggle against apartheid. His life was a lesson in selfless sacrifice, devotion to cause and stoic endurance. Morality and courage came together in his personality to offer hope to millions who chafed under oppressive regimes around the world.

Born into a clan chief's household in the Transkei region, Mandela formulated an anti–colonial and anti–racist outlook early in life. Fascinated by oral histories of South Africa before the advent of the Europeans, the young Mandela noted: 'Then the country was our own before the white people came, each clan lived in peace with the other clans.' Right from teen, Mandela understood the tricks of history. The British managed to conquer his land through divide–and–rule and dehumanised natives as inferior beings. His overriding mission was to regain ubuntu (humanity) for all South Africans through self–determination.

In the 1940s, Mandela solidified African nationalist ideology in the company of Walter Sisulu, Oliver Tambo and other Johannesburg activists who formed the kernel of the African National Congress' (ANC's) Youth League. He preferred mass action using nonviolent methods, thanks to the influence of Mahatma Gandhi's efforts for India's independence. He also believed that the brutal apartheid regime could be practically matched only through soul force. If resistance was not properly guided, it would end in frustration and disaster. However, Mandela did vacillate about the effectiveness of passive resistance at various junctures in the ANC's fight against the tyrannical white–minority government. The champion of peace could also be a man of war who approved of militancy in dire circumstances. A pragmatist at heart, he always attempted to veer the ANC towards strategies that worked to move the goal of liberation forward.

Mandela was a formidable grassroots organiser. He succeeded in converting ANC into a party with nationwide membership. Realising the importance of forging a multi–racial platform to resist apartheid, he built bridges with liberal whites, Indians and communists in a bid to unify South Africa. Chiefs in rural areas, many of whom collaborated with the Europeans and oppressed poor blacks, were also corralled into the umbrella coalition against racism. In travels across Africa, he enlisted international sympathy and support against apartheid.

▶An incomparable icon

Previous page: and opposite: Nelson Mandela transited from freedom fighter to elder statesman of the world with ease in the late nineties and well into the new millennium. His broad international humanism was reflected in several attempts to broker peace deals among warring countries and he continues to assist in raising awareness of oppressed people.

In 1958, Mandela married Winnie Madikizela, a radical social worker who played a flamboyant and controversial role in the anti-apartheid struggle. Her tenacity and love for the poor endeared her to many. Like Mandela, Winnie was the target of the colonial state's banning orders, arrests and crackdowns. Despite the couple's separation in 1992, Mandela acknowledged Winnie's contribution in his long walk to freedom: 'She was an indispensable pillar of support and comfort to myself personally.'

Mandela was undaunted by governmental efforts to break him down by depriving him of personal liberty, family and familiar creature comforts. His forbearance was exemplified by an oft-repeated self-affirmation: 'I had not chosen the path. The path had chosen me.' While all previous detentions of Mandela lasted for short to medium durations, in 1963, he was sentenced to life incarceration on charges of violent sabotage to attain political ends for heading a 'Communist organisation.' He was kept in inhuman conditions in Robben Island prison, now a pilgrimage site for all tourists to South Africa, for the next 27 years. Describing the gruesome indignities heaped on him and his compatriots, Mandela wrote: 'The prison operates to break the human spirit, to undermine human strength and destroy initiative.' A year later, when Mandela became South Africa's decision maker, penal system reform was high on his agenda.

Mandela's thoughts, letters and writings were smuggled out of prison throughout his jail term, electrifying the masses and drawing global attention. Starting in 1979, numerous human rights and peace awards were conferred on him in absentia, outside South Africa.

The world's most famous prisoner had songs, streets and parks named after him in far-flung corners. There was no greater symbol of freedom and human thirst for dignity. In 1985, Mandela was offered conditional release if he forsook planning and instigating 'Violence for the fur-

therance of political objectives.' It was the time-tested ploy of softening up a revolutionary by detaining him for decades and then offering him a 'Reprieve'. The lion hearted 67-year-old refused to compromise.

Eventually, international opprobrium, sanctions and relentless ANC pressure resulted in Mandela's release in 1990, followed by a gradual relaxation of apartheid and ushering in of majority rule in South Africa. In 1993, as an honour to his indomitable spirit and in recognition of his attempt to cure the cancer of apartheid peacefully, Mandela was awarded the Nobel Peace Prize along with his sagacious negotiator, President F.W. de Klerk. Mandela was unanimously chosen the first President of the new Republic after the 1994 multi-party elections.

President Mandela transited from freedom fighter to elder statesman of the world with ease in the late nineties. His broad international humanism was reflected in several attempts to broker peace deals among warring countries. He eschewed the apartheid regime's nuclear weapons and prevented any 'Reverse genocide' against the white minorities. His South Africa marched into a multi-racial horizon where the rights of all were respected. The maker of modern South Africa ensured that the hatreds of the past would not be made the basis for state policy. To this end, he wrote: 'To make peace with an enemy, one must work with that enemy, and then the enemy becomes your partner.'

Mandela continues to inspire by dint of his remarkable deeds in the service of humanity. The skill with which he steadied the ship of independent South Africa after 1994 cannot be understated, given the numerous fiascos confronted by newly liberated African countries. A tolerant, stable and democratic South Africa that responsibly leads African and third world affairs is a tribute to Mandela's farsightedness. Freedom fighter and nation-builder rolled into one, Mandela remains an incomparable icon.

Sir Winston Churchill

1874 – 1965

Britain's greatest saviour

British statesman and soldier, Winston Churchill, who came from a famous family, was one of the greatest orators of the twentieth century. His ease and facility of use of the English language and idiom were exemplary. A man who expanded a new-fangled 'Dialect,' in his own 'Write,' with expressions such as 'Blood, toil, tears, and sweat,' or 'The iron curtain' – a simile for the erstwhile Soviet Union, Churchill had few peers.

First educated at Harrow, Churchill graduated from Sandhurst. He began his military career and was appointed a Sub-Lieutenant in 1895. Churchill was soon assigned as 'Observer' to an anti-revolutionary Spanish force in Cuba, where he first saw military action. He was also posted in Bangalore, India, following which his assignments took him to the Tirah and the Nile Expeditionary Force, during which he was part of a celebrated cavalry charge.

Churchill was also a journalist beyond compare. His despatches were as prolific as his intellect. He was war correspondent for 'The London Daily Telegraph,' and wrote for the 'The Pioneer,' India. He also reported for 'The London Morning Post.' Following the onset of the Boer War, Churchill went to South Africa. He was taken prisoner by Louis Botha. His daring escape made him a front-page hero; but, beyond the call of duty, Churchill also became Botha's close friend.

Churchill followed his African experience with a lecture-sojourn of the U.S.. The trip rejuvenated him, and helped fund the beginning of a career in politics – his tryst with destiny. His first foray as a Conservative was a debacle; his next plunge, in 1900, was productive. Always the rebel, Churchill soon found himself in disagreement with the views of his colleagues. This led him to embrace the free-trade Liberals.

His political acumen and career now began to rise, and it predictably led to his getting Cabinet positions and also appointment as Privy chief. In 1908, Churchill became President of the Board of Trade and Home Secretary. In that capacity, Churchill pioneered progressive legislation including the establishment of the British Labour Exchange, pension for the aged, health and unemployment indemnity.

Churchill became the First Admiral in 1911. He began to arm the British armada for any eventuality, especially with Germany. When the Great War unleashed its terror, the Royal Navy quickly defeated the German navy. Confined as they were to their home-ports, the Germans began to now rely heavily on their submarine fleet.

Britain's greatest saviour

Previous page: The greatest public figure of his century, what made Churchill extraordinary was his incredible energy, vision, mind's eye, and daring bulldog tenacity. Opposite: Churchill from the outset was resolute on Hitler's total, unconditional surrender and planned for Britain to fight alone.

Churchill was also instrumental in powering the Royal Air Force, but what came as a bolt from the blue was his failed Dardanelles (Turkish) campaign. Churchill's plan misfired, and resulted in heavy casualties for the British. He was not only made a scapegoat; he was also relegated. He resigned from organisational service and opted to go to the front as a Lieutenant–Colonel. But, as luck would have it, he was called back by Lloyd George, the Prime Minister, and appointed Minister of Armaments.

Following the end of World War I, Churchill introduced a number of military reforms as Secretary of State for War and Air. He also became Secretary for the British–ruled Colonies. He worked towards the organisation of new Arab states, and a Jewish homeland in the Middle East, not to speak of a Free Irish State. But, his anti–socialist outlook brought him at loggerheads with the pro–labour section of the Liberal party. To add to the antipathy, Churchill lost the confidence of Lloyd George when he used British troops to suppress the Bolshevist regime in the Soviet Union (1924). However, he soon returned as a Conservative. He was quickly named Chancellor of the Exchequer, a position he had lost in the wake of his Russian 'Misadventure.'

Churchill was out of office, up until the beginning of World War II. Following public demand, he was reappointed First Lord of the Admiralty in September 1939. When Neville Chamberlain, who thought Herr Adolf Hitler was an honourable man, lost his premiership, in May 1940, Churchill became Prime Minister. When France fell to the Nazis, Churchill gallantly proclaimed in his first speech: 'You ask, what is our aim? I can answer in one word. Victory – victory at all costs, victory in spite of all terror; victory, however long and hard the road may be.'

Churchill from the outset was resolute on Hitler's total, unconditional surrender and planned for Britain to fight alone. When the U.S. entered the war, he changed his stance somewhat – albeit his commitment to bomb Germany and converge forces in the Mediterranean and the Middle East remained as firm as the Rock of Gibraltar. He once said: 'There is one thing that will bring Hitler down, and that is an absolutely devastating, exterminating attack by very heavy bombers from this country upon the Nazi homeland.' The landing in North Africa, followed by the invasion of Italy, were the very apotheosis of that view, juxtaposed by RAF's pounding of Germany with her bombers when Britain fought the battle almost single–handedly.

Churchill was no financial wizard; he followed conventional economics. He ended nationalisation of the steel and auto industries. Despite his disapproval, he also preserved some of the socialist measures initiated by the Labour government. However, he strongly opposed India's national movement for freedom. A hero after World War II, Churchill also donned the role of peace–time opposition leader.

The greatest public figure of his century, what made Churchill extraordinary was his incredible energy, vision, mind's eye, and daring bulldog tenacity. While his brilliant understanding evidenced by his superlative war leadership made him a colossal leader in his own right, critics often resented him for his colonial mind–set – the will to maintain Britain as a great power and an equally great state.

Knighted in 1953, Churchill, Britain's greatest saviour in shining valour, was awarded the Nobel Prize for Literature the same year. He retired from public life in 1955, but continued to retain a seat in Parliament till 1964.

F.W. de Klerk

1936 –

End of apartheid

Frederik Willem de Klerk was the politician–statesman of South Africa who sacrificed his own power to set in motion a chain of events that dismantled the edifice of apartheid and founded a multiracial democracy. Comparable to Mikhail Gorbachev of the former Soviet Union, de Klerk pulled the rug from under his own feet for the sake of South Africa's future. Booed by champions of apartheid as suicidal, de Klerk's course ultimately emancipated the enslaved black population and earned him a special niche in history as the liberal who defied his racist support base.

'Politics was in my blood', de Klerk declared in his autobiography. He was born in Johannesburg into a family closely involved in the origins of Afrikaner (Dutch settler) nationalism and its struggle for freedom from the British Empire. His grandfather was a founding member of the National Party that endeavoured to make South Africa a republic free from the British crown. His mentor and role model father was cabinet minister thrice in National Party governments and President of the Senate.

de Klerk had a very unsettled childhood due to the frequent career swings of his father, a poor schoolteacher in Transvaal region who rose in prominence into a top politi-

co. In his early days, de Klerk literally counted his pennies and picked and sold fruit for pocket money. His mother tutored the importance of being considerate to the less privileged, a lesson he extended to black children who were playmates on his farmland.

de Klerk was a frail boy often attacked by illness. At an all–Afrikaner boarding school, he negotiated with teachers the postponement of tests and other concessions on behalf of the rest of his classmates. He mobilised friends to join the youth wing of the National Party, following the family tradition. de Klerk approved of apartheid as a youth. Afrikaners were afraid of being swamped by the vast black majority if the controlling instrument of apartheid was removed. 'We were products of our times and circumstances', he reminisced later. At the age of thirteen, he contributed to his father's first election campaign for the Provincial Council.

Since an impressionable age, de Klerk wanted to be a lawyer 'As a brave defender of the truth.' He attended the conservative Potchefstroom University for an L.L.B degree. At college, he felt unease at the slow progress in self–government for South Africa's blacks, but stuck to the National party line that the African National Congress (ANC) and other revolutionaries were 'Terrorists.'

LEADERS & REVOLUTIONARIES

▶ End of apartheid

Previous page: Frederik Willem de Klerk was the politician–statesman of South Africa who dismantled the edifice of apartheid and founded a multiracial democracy. Opposite: In 1993, de Klerk reached an epic agreement with the ANC for transition to majority rule, an achievement that landed him and Mandela the Nobel Peace Prize.

He married co-student Marike and went on to set up a thriving corporate law firm in Vereeneging in 1959. Over the next twelve years, de Klerk cultivated local political contact networks that came in handy when he stood for parliament from the same town. His diligent efforts for promoting Afrikaner language and culture paved the way to election as an MP in 1972.

As MP, de Klerk was the National Party's spokesman on labour matters. Labelled 'Young Turk', he backed recognition of black trade unions. In 1978, he was made minister of telecommunications and welfare, heralding an 11 year stint as cabinet member. de Klerk served tenures as minister for sports, home affairs, minerals and education, winning a reputation for reformism and taking on entrenched interests. One measure he got legislated against strident white antagonism was increasing expenditure on black education. His role as peacemaker and bridge–builder between rival National Party factions in the early eighties attracted national media attention. A liberal who barely hid contempt for his hawkish boss, President P.W. Botha, de Klerk vowed quietly to himself 'That I would change his dictatorial style if I ever became President.'

Minister de Klerk was troubled by conscience at the injustices being heaped on blacks and Indians by the Pretoria regime of which he was part. Yet, he dutifully toed the official stand that ANC had to forsake violence to deserve negotiation. He was not privy to the 'Total Onslaught' of Botha that committed grave crimes against humanity (including alleged chemical and biological warfare on poor blacks). de Klerk's basic Christian belief was that governments must uphold human rights and justice.

Elected President in 1989, de Klerk normalised the mandate of security forces that had gone berserk under Botha. He arranged a secret meeting with the jailed leader, Nelson Mandela, and struck a famous equation with him.

Mandela and a host of other resistance fighters were released in succession and the ANC ban was removed. In 1991, de Klerk passed legislation that repealed racially discriminatory laws affecting residence, education, public amenities, and health care. Realising the value of consensus within the ruling class for far–reaching relaxations, he won a referendum from white South Africans in 1992 to continue liberalising.

In 1993, de Klerk reached an epic agreement with the ANC for transition to majority rule, an achievement that landed him and Mandela the Nobel Peace Prize. He had proved his favourite maxim that 'Even the most intractable problems can be resolved through compromise, negotiations and goodwill.' In 1994, de Klerk joined Nelson Mandela's historic Government of National Unity as Deputy President and oversaw a smooth transition to democracy.

After quitting office in 1996 and heading the opposition for a year, de Klerk retired from politics in 1997. He appealed for the replacement of race oriented with value oriented politics. His greatest regret was failure to secure a 'Power sharing model' during the negotiations with ANC, which in his opinion could have prevented majoritarian policies that marginalised significant minorities.

In retrospect, de Klerk was accused of making virtue out of necessity by critics who thought that the new internal and international environments rendered apartheid unsustainable in the early nineties. However, his pragmatism, patience and tolerance had a crucial influence on crafting the endgame of minority rule. He read the writing on the wall and took corrective steps before disaster came in the form of civil war or economic collapse. An open mind who never shielded himself from new truths, de Klerk was, in Mandela's words, 'too honest' a human being to forsake principles.

Mahatma Gandhi

1869 – 1948

An inspirational leader

Mohandas Karamchand Gandhi, or, quite simply, Mahatma Gandhi the apostle of peace, was born in Porbandar, India on October 2nd 1869.

Gandhi's definition of religion, or spirituality, was a human activity – the everyday bustle of life. It was an aspiration that formed the underpinning, or near-failure of his childhood and youthful days, and his almost hesitant thrust into the struggle for equality in South Africa including the long drawn out non-violent, crusade for India's independence from British rule.

Following his none too eventful early education, Gandhi went to England to qualify at the bar which was the in-thing among well heeled Indians of the time. His preliminary step as a lawyer was disappointing. A new door opened for him in 1893 in South Africa. He signed a contract in connection with a civil suit. Soon, Gandhi began to get his first taste of racial discrimination and hapless compliance of Indian settlers. That he was once unceremoniously thrown out of a train for having travelled with a valid first–class ticket, an only White prerogative, was another 'Salvo.' The ignominy only intensified his resolve. When the Natal Legislature began to tinker with a bill to disfranchise Indian migrants, Gandhi lost no time in planning a resistance. This was his first political campaign, with which he instilled a new fortitude of unity. His movement brought home the connotations of the draconian act. In the process, it transformed Gandhi from a reluctant hero to a seasoned campaigner, and also helped him to organise the heterogeneous Indian community into a cohesive unit. He called it Ashram.

Soon enough, the means of access to the discriminatory Asiatic Registration Act in Transvaal (1907) stirred Gandhi to formulate a new method of protest and petition. It was a silver–lining in the dark clouds that loomed large following Gandhi's long struggle for 'Equal' rights, which had produced no result. Gandhi called his novel plan Passive Resistance, or Satyagraha, a movement devoid of both verbal and physical violence, even in the face of brutality. It had South Africa, and the civilised world, thinking.

In 1915, Gandhi, who was greatly motivated by some of India's great nationalist leaders, returned to his homeland. In so doing, he had given up a flourishing future and, his much–loved community work. He was given a hero's welcome but, politics was still a distant thought in his mind. That however changed in 1917. Gandhi went to Champaran, the indigo–growing district in Eastern India, and took up the cause of tenants against British

► An inspirational leader

Previous page: Following his none–too–eventful early education, Gandhi went to England to qualify at the bar – an in–thing among well–to–do Indians of the time. Opposite: India became independent on August 15, 1947, through peaceful means, thanks mainly due to Gandhi's non–violent movement.

planters. This was followed by his agitation for reduction of land tax in Kaira, where crops could not be grown due to failed rains. Gandhi fought causes that seemed to have a local bearing. He saw to it that they did not precipitate into a face–off with the British government in Delhi. This was his masterstroke but the British apparatus was imperiously 'Dismissive' of Gandhi's growing charisma.

Things came to a head when the government proposed to introduce a legislation (Rowlatt Bills) to curb civil liberties. Gandhi, who had supported Britain in its war–time efforts, felt betrayed. As India geared to oppose the measure without success, Gandhi felt very strongly that it was time to use his Satyagraha 'Spark' to build the fuel for non–violent resistance, and ensure the repeal of the Rowlatt Bills. He called for a nation–wide strike, a brilliant move as the whole of India came to a standstill. On the ugly side, there was violence in a few towns and cities. Gandhi was dismayed. He thought India was not yet ready for peaceful resistance.

Worse was yet to come when British troops fired on and massacred hundreds of guiltless men, women and children, who had assembled for a prayer meeting in the Punjab, it agonised the entire nation. Gandhi's alienation from British hegemony was now total. He concluded that the foreign system of governance and control of India had to end.

Gandhi immersed himself into the national movement for India's independence head–on by way of his extraordinary line of action – non–violence. He aroused the entire nation as a heaven–sent messiah. His radiant prescription for passive resistance encompassed the boycott of councils, courts, and schools, set up by the British – including foreign clothes. Gandhi's action plan began to paralyse the

British administration and the writing for the abdication of its throne in India was on the wall.

India became independent on August 15, 1947, through peaceful means, thanks mainly to Gandhi's non–violent movement. But, in the wake of euphoria, Gandhi was a sad man and witness to the untold tragedy of partition of his beloved country, based on religious lines – a Hindu India and Muslim Pakistan. The dissection soon ignited religious hatred and led to the slaughter of people in their millions on either side. The most diabolical in history. Yet, in the midst of anarchy, Gandhi found the strength to bring peace with his profound message of amity and mandatory fast.

The paradox of life had to catch up with Gandhi, a man of harmony. Hindu fundamentalists nursed a grouse. They felt that Gandhi had appeased the Muslims for too long. The spin–off came in the form of an assassin's bullet. It stilled the life of Gandhi, a seer like no other, at a prayer meeting in close proximity with his God.

Gandhi relentlessly recognised the bedlam when we deny our responsibility and proceed in pursuit of self–interest. He summarised our responsibility for each other in his Seven Social Sins, a keynote on how social evil can run: 1. politics without principle; 2. wealth without work; 3. commerce without morality; 4. pleasure without conscience; 5. education without character; 6. science without humanity; and, 7. worship without sacrifice.

Gandhi was an inspirational leader. To use a cliché, he was a truly great human being. What guided him was his conduct – a virtual obsession with character. He often said, 'We must be the change we wish to see in the world.' This was his legacy.

Mikhail Gorbachev

1931 -

Man of destiny

Born into a family of peasants, Mikhail Gorbachev, the man of destiny, studied law at Moscow University. He graduated in 1955. It was during his university days that he happened to meet and fall in love with Raisa. Following their wedding in 1953, the Gorbachevs shifted residence to Mikhail's home-town of Stavropol in Southern Russia. Gorbachev was only 21 when he joined the Communist Party of the Soviet Union (CPSU) in 1952.

His peasant genetics never deserted him. At the age of 35, in the midst of party activity, Gorbachev graduated from the Agricultural Institute as an agronomist and economist. It was only now that his career took off in earnest. His educational background helped him immensely in his pursuits including the dreams he may have had in mind. He was appointed First Secretary for Agriculture (1970). One year later, Gorbachev became a member of the Central Committee.

Gorbachev led a Soviet delegation to Belgium, in 1972. Two years later, he became a Representative to the Supreme Soviet. He was also now made Chairman of the Standing Commission on Youth Affairs. Five years later, he was promoted to the Politburo. It was here that he came under the tutelage of Yuri Andropov, Head of the KGB,

who saw more than a spark of genius in Gorbachev. Andropov, coincidentally was also a native of Stavropol. There was that local 'Bonding' too. Gorbachev was elevated as a leader of the Party before his mentor passed away in 1984.

Gorbachev oversaw responsibility on personnel in the party and outside, during his tenure under Andropov. The duo, in consonance and with full agreement, replaced one-third of the top brass in the government. This included ministers and regional governors. They began to repose more faith in youth. It was also during this time that Grigory Romanov, Nikolai Ryzhkov and Yegor Ligachev became prominent, the last two for their understanding of economics and personnel, respectively.

Gorbachev was also quite liked by Konstantin Chernenko, who succeeded Andropov. Gorbachev served him as Second Secretary. However, what broadened his outlook and horizons were the travel opportunities he could muster thanks to his influence within the CPSU. This was to deeply affect his political and societal views in the future as head of his country.

Following the death of Chernenko, Gorbachev was elected General Secretary of the Communist Party (1985). It was a record of sorts in the Soviet Union, which always

▶ Man of destiny

Previous page: Through Gorbachev's policy of glasnost the Soviets were given greater freedom of speech, Opposite: In September 2004, while in London, Gorbachev declared 'That war on Iraq was a mistake. It not only undermined international law, it undermined democracy. '

had a clear spot for older people to head the country's top political posts. Gorbachev was just 54 – what's more, he also became the Party's first leader to be born in the aftermath of the Russian Revolution (1917).

Thanks to the knowledge and insight he had gained by way of his foreign trips, Gorbachev took some bold decisions (1986). He launched the big initiative to reform the festering communist rule and the state economy. He also introduced 'glasnost' (openness), 'Perestroika' (restructuring') and 'Uskorenie' (accelerated economic development) – the first two words became not only popular expressions, but also oft-repeated idioms in the world.

Gorbachev was convinced that his economic reforms would not only raise living standards, but also increase worker productivity. He brought in The Law on Co-operatives, a hugely radical concept which allowed private ownership of businesses in the services, manufacturing, restaurants, shops, and foreign-trade sectors. Although the model, at first, levied steep duty and employment limitations, it brought in new enthusiasm for growth in the Soviet psyche. The face of the Soviet Union, the land behind the iron curtain, was now changing.

Through Gorbachev's policy of glasnost the Soviets were given greater freedom of speech, which was in sharp contrast to the era of Josef Stalin and the leaders that came after him. The press began to breathe fresh, free air. They also began to air their views without trepidation. Most importantly, Gorbachev released hundreds of political prisoners and dissidents in the mood of glasnost.

Gorbachev now began to focus his energies on democratisation of the government apparatus. In June 1988, he launched radical reforms to reduce party control of the government machinery. His landmark resolution was ratified and a dazzling new chapter had emerged from an epoch of darkness.

Gorbachev was just as far-reaching and practical in international affairs. He met U.S. President Ronald Reagan and discussed reducing Intermediate-Range Nuclear Weapons in Europe. The commitment on both sides led to the initialisation of the Intermediate-Range Nuclear Forces (INF) Treaty (1987). The following year, Gorbachev announced the withdrawal of Soviet forces from Afghanistan.

Gorbachev also departed from the Leonid Brezhnev Doctrine, and allowed the Eastern Bloc nations to establish their own internal affairs. The result was immediate – Eastern Europe was transformed. Communism had collapsed, with the exception of Romania. It was a peaceful transition brought about by the steely tenacity and courage of one man. In the process, the Cold War Age was dumped into the dustbin of history. Needless to say, Gorbachev was awarded the Nobel Peace Prize in 1990.

The spill over of Gorbachev's Herculean efforts also led to the undermining of the Soviet Union and the man himself. Nationalist zeal compounded by unrest in the Soviet Republics of Georgia, Ukraine, Kazakhstan, Armenia, Azerbaijan etc., came to the forefront. This, sooner than later, knocked the underbelly of the Soviet Union and, resulted in its demolition.

The old brigade in the Soviet leadership organised a coup (1991) to remove Gorbachev from power. He was held in captivity and later freed. Curiously, Gorbachev found that he had lost his hold, and the pendulum of power was now in the hands of his nationalist rival, Boris Yeltsin.

In September 2004, while in London, Gorbachev declared 'That war on Iraq was a mistake. It not only undermined international law, it undermined democracy. Millions spoke out, but the war was launched in spite of their democratic views.'

Mao Tse Tung

1893 – 1976

The birth of China

Mao Tse Tung was born in Hunan Province to a peasant family. He served in the provincial army, and became an ardent advocate of physical fitness, co-operative and united action.

Mao graduated in 1918, and travelled to Beijing during the May Fourth Movement, with his teacher and father–in–law, who lectured at Peking University. On the latter's recommendation, Mao began to work in the university library. It was here that he developed an avid interest in reading and, in the process, married Yang Kaihui, a student.

Mao did not wish to go abroad for learning or education. Instead, he began to travel all over China. He returned to Hunan, and began his work to promote collective action and labour rights – his long abiding passion.

Mao attended the First Congress of the Communist Party of China in Shanghai in 1921. He was elected to the Central Committee of the party at the Third Congress, two years later. He also served as the head of the Kuomintang's (KMT) or Nationalist Party Peasant Training Institute. He made a good impression, and was sent to Hunan Province to report on the peasant revolt. This laid the foundation for Maoist theory.

Slowly, Mao developed many of his political theories. His ideas were significant, albeit not original. But, his thoughts were to considerably influence generations of Chinese and the rest of the world, the foremost among them was his view of the peasant being the embodiment of revolution. It was a brilliant stroke, because China had no major urban working–class population; also, its huge peasant population were a disgruntled lot. This was the right platform for communism to take its bow in the country.

Mao derived much of his early thought from the works of Hegel and Marx. He created a new theory of materialist dialectics. He applied the theory to real world conflicts and also initiated a three–stage hypothesis of guerrilla warfare and the premise of a people's democratic dictatorship.

Mao led the doomed Autumn Harvest Uprising at Changsha, Hunan. He survived the misadventure, and escaped execution by the skin of his teeth. He took refuge in the mountains. In the years that followed, he helped establish the Chinese Soviet Republic. Needless to say, he was elected Chairman. He also married He Zizhen, after his first wife was killed by government forces. A visionary, Mao now began to build an effective guerrilla force. Side-by-side, he indulged himself in rural reform and administration. He provided a sanctuary for communists

▶ The birth of China

Previous page: Mao announced the emergence of the People's Republic of China on October 1, 1949.
Opposite: The Long March between 1934 and 1935 saved Mao and the Communist Party from the attacks by the Guomingdang.

running away from rightist 'Cleansing' in the cities. However, a swift struggle for communist leadership led to him being ousted from his important position. He was replaced by those thought to be friendly by Moscow, which was not the case. This included future Prime Minister, Zhou Enlai.

Chiang Kai–shek, who, during the interregnum, had developed some clout, and nominal control of China, was keen to liquidate the communists and their ideology. To elude the KMT forces, the communists now engaged in the 'Long March' – from Jiangxi in the South–East to Shaanxi in North–West China. This was a mammoth 9,600km, year–long journey. Mao now emerged as a communist leader with immense appeal.

Mao led the communist battle against the Japanese in the Sino–Japanese War (1937–1945), with courage and tactical acumen. He was not supported in his efforts by the U.S. He became a hero of sorts and this helped him to further consolidate power within the Communist Party. He engineered the 'Rectification' campaign, in 1942, and also married actress Lan Ping, later Jiang Qing.

The U.S. continued to support Chiang Kai–shek to crush communism. On the other hand, the Soviet Union embraced Mao and gave him arms to keep Chiang Kai-shek away from consolidating power. When KMT troops suffered huge loses against Mao's forces, in 1949, the communists laid siege to Chengdu, the final KMT–occupied frontier in mainland China. Chiang Kai–shek fled to Taiwan.

Mao announced the emergence of the People's Republic of China on October 1, 1949. He had now defeated both the Japanese and the KMT. He was the Chairman of PRC from 1954 to 1959, and took up residence in Zhongnanhai, a complex adjacent to the Forbidden City in Beijing. He

terminated the laying of a swimming pool in the vicinity as being in violation of his austere living.

Mao got into the thick of activity and fuelled the engines of China's progress though rapid, forced collectivisation. He introduced price control measures and held inflation at bay. Inflation, till this point of time, was a Chinese bugbear. He also introduced land reforms, and led China to sustained GDP growth of about 4.9 per cent. Life not only improved in the country, it also led to all–round progress. His government did its part for the promotion of science, women's and minorities' rights and dealt with drug abuse and prostitution with an iron hand.

Mao also pursued the 'Hundred Flowers' campaign – a collection of diverse views as to how China should be governed. It was an idea that failed, because there were opinions expressed that did not brighten Mao's or his party's fame. However, Mao launched the Great Leap Forward, in 1958. It was a model for economic growth which was agriculture-centric, not industry–oriented. It was a disaster that led to a great famine and deaths of millions of people.

It was around this time that the Soviet Union and China slowly began to part; the two did not see eye–to–eye. The Chinese economy also began to wobble. There was some dissent within the party for Mao's high–handedness. Top members of the party now felt it was time for him to 'Renounce' power. This included Liu Shaoqi, and the moderate Deng Xiaoping.

Mao countered in typical fashion. He launched the Cultural Revolution in 1966. This led to the demolition of China's cultural heritage and incarceration of a large number of intellectuals. However, sooner than later, Mao's deteriorating health put the spoke in his political wheel. He was noiselessly sidelined. It was a silent farewell to a great revolutionary.

Richard Nixon

1913 – 1994

Watergate dishonour

Richard Nixon was born in Yorba Linda, California. He graduated from Whittier College, California, and Duke University School of Law in Durham, in the late–1930s. A brilliant advocate, Nixon became a partner in a law firm, soon after. He enrolled in the U.S. Navy, during World War II, and served in the Pacific. At the end of the war, Nixon was promoted to Lieutenant Commander.

Nixon was the President of the U.S. from 1969 to 1974. The only U.S. President ever to resign from office, while facing impeachment for his involvement in the (in)famous Watergate political scandal, Nixon was, indeed, a man of many parts with a steely resolve. He held onto his own ground or conviction without flinching, never ever showing an iota of vulnerability. He would hold his nerve somehow and, always presented a cold countenance.

In 1946, Nixon made his debut in politics. He won a seat in the U.S. House of Representatives, following a belligerent campaign. His premise was an absolute, unrelenting antipathy towards communism. A Republican through and through, Nixon was re–elected to the House in 1948. Two years later, he was elected to the Senate. Nixon also donned the role of Vice–President under President Dwight D. Eisenhower.

During his initial tenure as President, Nixon created a roadmap for the successful resolution of the Vietnam War. This led to the gradual withdrawal of U.S. troops from Vietnam. Further to this, Nixon also became instrumental in easing the long–drawn tensions that existed between the U.S., Mao's China, and the Soviet Union. His landmark visit to China, in 1972, made him the first U.S. President to visit that country. He followed his Chinese voyage with a visit to the Soviet Union, yet another groundbreaking sojourn. This finally led to Congressional approval of U.S.–Soviet accords to limit the production of nuclear weapons and a mood of détente between the two super-powers and arch–rivals.

Nixon was on song with his three major triumphs so too, was his government. However, the Watergate scandal emerged from a political larceny at the Democratic National Headquarters in the Watergate Building in Washington, knocking the reputation of his government. This was just one among several other illegal activities made by employees of Nixon's 1972 re–election campaign. Nixon went into action and tried his best to hide his alleged crimes. This was the beginning of his end – a shameful saga that led to the move for his impeachment.

A stubborn customer, Nixon did not at first heed several legal requests to turn over his secret tape recordings of conversations at the White House. He slowly relented and handed over the tapes. The tapes revealed that Nixon had given the go–ahead for a 'Cover–up' within a week following the Watergate crime. He now faced imminent impeachment at the House of Representatives and removal from office by the Senate. On August 9, 1974, Nixon resigned. Vice–President Gerald Ford took oath as President. This was a quirk of fate, or political diversion. In September, Ford had granted Nixon a pardon – virtually freeing Nixon from 'Burglary' of all federal crimes that his ex–boss may have committed as President.

Nixon had his share of achievements as a President–Statesman. To name a few; revenue sharing, new anti–crime laws, and a broad environmental programme. He also appointed Justices of Conservative Philosophy to the Supreme Court. His most dramatic moment, however, emerged when U.S. astronauts successfully achieved their first landing on the Moon, in 1969.

Henry Kissinger

1923 -

A negotiator par excellence

Henry Kissinger was born in Germany into a Jewish family. His family fled the country at the height of Adolf Hitler's campaign of terror. He became a naturalised American citizen in 1943.

Kissinger attended night school, in Washington, and worked during the day. When he attended college, he enlisted in the army, thanks to his German accent, which has always resided in him. He became a German interpreter for the U.S. Intelligence Corps.

As Nixon's National Security Adviser (1969–73), and Secretary of State (1973–74), Kissinger continued in the latter capacity with President Gerald Ford (1974–77). It was during his tenure with Nixon that Kissinger formulated the policy of détente with the Soviets. He also played a key role in the Strategic Arms Limitation Talks and the Anti–Ballistic Missile Treaty.

Kissinger went to the People's Republic of China to confer with Premier Zhou Enlai secretly. His two visits set the platform for Nixon's landmark visit to China (1972) and stabilisation of relations between the two giants. He had now built a huge reputation for himself – a negotiator par excellence.

The winner of the 1973 Nobel Peace Prize, Kissinger and Nixon had promised a swift end to the Vietnam War in the election manifesto. However, the first few years of Nixon's presidentship saw only the intensification of the bloody conflict, which did not do America proud.

However, one of Kissinger's finest hours came when he parleyed for the end of the Yom Kippur War, which was triggered following Egypt's invasion of the Sinai, juxtaposed by Syria's incursion of the Golan Heights. But, all was not fair on another front – it is said that Kissinger played a quiet role in the coup that disposed the government of Chilean President Salvador Allende.

Critics also imply that Kissinger was a master of deception and initiated several devious moves in foreign countries. However, he was quite popular within the U.S. and emerged as a much–liked man in the otherwise debased Nixon government. That he was not involved in the Watergate scandal which rocked and displaced Nixon was another factor that helped him to come clean, despite the fact that he was often seen as a debonair diplomat. But, what disturbed his standing was his alleged covert support to President Suharto of Indonesia for the invasion of East Timor. The perfidious attack led to a brutal massacre of over 200,000 Timorese. Kissinger played down his role saying that he was unaware of Suharto's plan.

When Ford lost the 1976 elections to Jimmy Carter, Kissinger left office. When President George Bush appointed Kissinger to a key position to investigate the terrorist attack on the World Trade Center of September 11, 2001, his appointment was not well received. The position did not entitle him to any remuneration. He resigned from the commission alluding to variance of concerns with his clients.

For a long–time public figure, Kissinger has been accused of conspiracy, murder, and other transgressions – including war crimes. Critics cite that it was Kissinger who directed the first part of unlawful and covert U.S. bombings in Cambodia (1969–1975), which resulted in over 210,000 casualties. It is also said that he tacitly accepted West Pakistan's ethnic cleansing in East Pakistan (now Bangladesh) against Bengalis, during the Third Indo–Pakistani War only due to the overt fact that the non–democratic and military–ruled Pakistan was a loyal U.S. Cold War partner. Observers also believe that Kissinger connived in a successful Greek Cypriot coup, not to speak of a failed 'Subterfuge' in Turkey.

Twice married, Kissinger is today the chief of Kissinger and Associates, his own consulting organisation.

Margaret Thatcher

1925 –

The iron lady of politics

Margaret Thatcher's father was a politician as well as a grocer. Politics, it was, and not cuisine, that silhouetted Margaret's mindscape from her formative years. She excelled in school, and went to Oxford. Her subject was chemistry. After obtaining a degree, she worked as a chemist and formulated a process that preserved icecream.

In 1950, she fought her first election and won a seat from Dartford and became the youngest woman to do so. A rising star, her activity was as impressive as her ideology. She soon came in contact with Denis Thatcher, a wealthy businessman. It was love at first sight, and the rest is history. Thatcher qualified as a Barrister in 1953, and also specialised in taxation.

Slowly, she began to look for a safe Conservative seat, and it was only in 1959, after many rejections, that she was given a ticket. She easily won the seat and also crusaded for a Bill in her maiden speech, which forced local councils to hold meetings in public. She became Parliamentary Secretary at the Ministry of Pensions and National Insurance in September 1961. When Sir Alec Douglas–Home stepped down, she supported the ascendancy of Edward Heath. She joined the Shadow Treasury Team in 1966.

Thatcher supported a Bill to make male homosexuality legal. She was one among a few that took the contentious stand. She also voted in favour of another Bill that legalised abortion. Paradoxically, she opposed the abolition of capital punishment.

She now spoke with panache, and it was not long before she was made Shadow Fuel Spokesman in 1967, and promoted to Shadow Transport, and finally Education, before the general elections (1970).

When Heath was elected Prime Minister, Thatcher became Secretary of State for Education and Science, and quickly established herself in the news. She 'Formalised' a slash in the Education Budget, and abolished the supply of free milk in schools. She became known as 'Maggie Thatcher, milk snatcher,' but she also promulgated an all–inclusive secondary education, without cutting the Open University budgetary allocation.

Following the defeat of her party, four years later, Thatcher continued to be in the limelight and when she became Leader of the Opposition (1976), she made a stirring speech and ridiculed the Soviet Union for 'Putting guns before butter.' Touchy as her sermon was, it gave her a great deal of publicity. The Soviet newspaper, 'Red Star' gave her what was to become a permanent sobriquet –

The iron lady of politics

Previous page: Thatcher was a champion of the free market economy and entrepreneurship. She also pursued a policy of privatisation.
Opposite: In 1978, Thatcher became England's first–ever woman Prime Minister and took her country's economic slide head–on, and turned it around.

'Iron Lady.' She delighted in the expression and carried it with élan all through her political career and beyond.

In 1978, Thatcher shifted her concern to Britain's immigration policy. She spoke with gusto saying that immigrants were 'Flooding' Britain. She raised a storm, and she also got the votes. She became England's first–ever woman Prime Minister and took her country's economic slide head–on, and turned it around. Next, she made her presence felt in international politics and also increased Britain's interest rates to pin down inflation. It was a move that hit businesses below the belt, and brought in an upsurge of unemployment.

Thatcher's mind–set was keyed to the supply–side of economics; it was not recession–centric. Whenever her popularity was slightly on the edge, she rallied around, and often said that she would not make an about face. When Argentine forces invaded the Falkland Islands (1982), a British territory, Thatcher sent a naval task force which defeated the Argentines. This was god–sent; she became an emblem of British patriotic fervour which resulted in a landslide victory for the Conservatives in the general elections (1983). She once again took the plunge into controversy with her 'Right to Buy' – a policy that authorised residents of Council Housing to buy their homes at a markdown.

No admirer of trade unions, Thatcher also formulated incremental change rather than a single Act. The trade unions went on the rampage. Always the tough lady with a prescient mind, Thatcher had made provisions for coal stocks. She saw to it that there were no cuts in electric power. She smartly managed to swing public opinion again in her favour. The coal miners relented. They had no choice.

In 1984, Thatcher miraculously escaped an attempt on her life. This happened in the midst of her stoical stance against the unions. It brought her into the forefront of

political visibility again. To prove her point, that nothing could really hobble her undertaking, she spoke at a Conference even before the debris at the site of the bomb explosion was cleared.

Thatcher was a champion of the free market economy and entrepreneurship. She also pursued a policy of privatisation. This was called 'Thatcherism', a popular concept that has spread far across the world.

A political soul mate of U.S. President Ronald Reagan, Thatcher was an ardent supporter of U.S. policies of preclusion against the Soviet Union, during the Cold War. She also permitted the U.S. the use of British bases, and invited protests from bodies and groups that supported nuclear disarmament. She allowed the U.S. bombing on Libya from bases in Britain in 1986, and subsequently prevented the helicopter manufacturer Westland from tying–up with the Italian firm, Agusta. Instead, she favoured Westland's connection with Sikorsky Aircraft Corporation of the U.S.

The cut on education, which was now a part of her early days in politics, began to badger her. In 1985, the University of Oxford refused Thatcher an honourary degree – an award that is a prerogative for Prime Ministers who have been educated at the university.

Thatcher made two profound foreign policy decisions. She visited China and signed the Sino–British Joint Declaration for the handover of Hong Kong in 1997 and argued that Britain paid far more to the European Economic Community than it received in expenditure. She bargained for a budget 'Discount,' and emerged triumphant.

When Thatcher won the general elections, in 1987, she became the first Prime Minister of the United Kingdom to win three successive general elections since Lord Liverpool (1812–1827).

Anwar Sadat

1918 – 1981

Pioneer of peace

One of thirteen brothers and sisters, Mohamed Anwar el–Sadat, Egyptian politician and President (1970 to 1981), graduated from the Royal Military Academy in Cairo. He enrolled as an officer in a group committed to free Egypt from British rule.

Sadat was imprisoned twice by the British, during and after World War II: once, for his secret efforts to get 'Armed' help from the Nazi–Italian–Japanese Axis combined to turn the tables against the occupying British forces, and for his revolutionary activities, later. The boredom of prison led him to learn French and English. Following his release, Sadat switched to civilian life. He acted for a while, and ran a business. It was during one of his business assignments that he met Jihan and married her.

Sadat participated actively in the coup d'état that deposed King Farouk I (1952). He got into active politics, which came to him naturally, and after holding several key positions in the Egyptian government, he was made Vice–President in President Gamal Abdul Nasser's cabinet (1969). Nasser was Sadat's mentor. When Nasser died a shattered man, the following year, in the wake of a military debacle against Israel, Sadat succeeded him as President.

Three years later, Sadat entered into a 'Concordat' with Syria, and led Egypt in the Yom Kippur War with Israel. His objective was simple: he wanted to retrieve parts of the Sinai Peninsula, which had been occupied by Israel during the disastrous Six–Day War, which agonised Nasser enormously and precipitated his death. Israel did not flinch, and held on to its ground. But, Sadat's resolve in the face of tremendous odds helped revive Egypt's slumped self–esteem. This was, indeed, the precursor to the formulation of a peace settlement. It was a feather in Sadat's political cap and prudence, following which he came to be called the 'Hero of the Crossing.'

In the years ahead, Sadat's reputation as a statesman of international stature began to gain solid ground, and for good reasons. He became the first Arab leader to officially visit Israel. It was a historic moment, no less, when he met Israeli Prime Minister Menachem Begin, and spoke before the Israeli Parliament, Knesset (1977). It was not that Sadat made the Arab world happy by his visit – many within the Muslim world condemned his shaking hands with Begin as 'Capitulation'.

Sadat, who made the visit following an invitation from Begin sought a permanent peace settlement that would transform the Arab world, ease tensions in the Middle East, and bring hope to the region. It was a bold initiative, in the midst of discontent and raging emotion. Sadat's peace effort did not go in vain, notwithstanding the resentment it caused across the Suez. On the positive side, it led to the Camp David Peace Agreement. Sadat and Begin shared the Nobel Peace Prize for their co–ordinated and cohesive stand.

Sadat was assassinated during a parade in Cairo by armymen who were part of the Egyptian Islamic Jihad organisation, which had all along disagreed on his parleys with Israel, not to speak of his crackdown on Muslim organisations and fundamentalist forces. Sadat was succeeded by his Vice–President Hosni Mubarak and continues to rule Egypt with a firm hand.

Jawaharlal Nehru

1889 - 1964

India's great statesman

Jawaharlal Nehru, free India's first Prime Minister, was a great statesman, visionary, and idealist. Born in a wealthy, aristocratic family, Nehru studied in Harrow and at Cambridge. He became a lawyer, and joined the Bar in the Allahabad High Court.

Nehru came under the influence of Mahatma Gandhi, his mentor, and joined the Indian Congress Committee (1918). Imprisoned several times by the British during India's struggle for independence, Nehru was elected President of the Indian National Congress in 1929.

After he became Prime Minister (1947), Nehru followed a policy of neutrality during the Cold War. He introduced a policy of industrialisation, established institutes of science and technology, management, and science research centres – now India's pride. He reorganised India's princely states on linguistic lines, and brought the dispute with Pakistan over Kashmir to the U.N. A bold, albeit lopsided measure that could not produce détente. The wrangle continues to be locked in a battle of attrition on either side of the great divide even today.

A charismatic leader and a brilliant orator, Nehru venerated Gandhi but he was not so much drawn to Gandhi's ideal of an agrarian society. Nehru championed industrialisation and socialism for India, drawn as he was to the works of Karl Marx. However, the two great men were united to each other in their souls and espoused a common dream of a peaceful, secular, united, and great India.

Nehru ruled India for seventeen long years, and led it through many upheavals, which included the gigantic deluge of Hindu refugees from Pakistan during partition, a war with Pakistan, followed by the integration of the princely states into a new political structure.

Although he attracted controversy and bewilderment related to the reorganisation of Indian states on a linguistic foundation, just as much as he launched a series of five–year plans with the declared goal of achieving a 'Socialist pattern of society,' an inspiration he drew from the Soviet Union's 'Piatiletka' or 5–Year Plan, Nehru wanted the best of both worlds – a combination of socialism and capitalism to fuel India's drive to progress and self–sufficiency. While the Soviet Union fuelled India's path to progress and development of independent capabilities in many spheres of heavy industry, engineering, and cutting–edge technologies, Nehru deftly combined internal political freedom, economic and political independence and balanced India's relationship on both sides of the spectrum, the Eastern Bloc and the West.

▶ India's great statesman

Previous page: Nehru achieved so much that only a few can dream of in one's lifetime, but like all great men history has found him incomplete. Opposite: In foreign affairs, Nehru championed a policy of neutralism.

Critics lament the fact that Nehru's economics was faulty. But, the reality remains that he did what was in the best interests of the nation in his epoch. His idea of state intervention and investment was developed when transfer of capital and technology to India was not easily flowing from state–sponsored capital controls of the developed world. It was not quite like what it is today in Nehru's era, when the transfer of capital is easily channelled to recipient nations – more so in new, emerging markets.

Nehru's political philosophy was eclectic. It was a composite blend of nineteenth century liberalism, Fabian socialism, Marxist and Russian economics, and Gandhian ethics and Nehru's own reading and understanding of Indian aspirations and needs. No wonder, Nehru always wanted the state to be the principal entrepreneur, with all citizens being equal share holders. His outstanding achievement is mirrored in the democratic pillars he established at all levels.

In foreign affairs, Nehru championed a policy of neutralism. One of the architects of the non–aligned movement, Nehru opposed the formation of military alliances. He called for a 'Freeze' on all nuclear testing. He knew the implications of nuclear war. However, there were times when he discarded neutralism for a pro–Western policy. One prime example was his appeal for Western aid during the Chinese incursion on Indian soil in 1962.

Nehru had the uncanny knack of seeing several faces of a given problem quickly. It was an advantage and a disadvantage too – because, he would vacillate sometimes, and not take swift decisions. Fortunately, he was not dogmatic. He would modify his stand once he was certain that it was on the right lines. What dictated Nehru's politics was not merely intellectualism or a pursuit of power for the sake of power alone. His political beliefs emanated from his strong conviction and profound sense of concern for the underdog and a passion for world peace. Nehru thought of himself as a global citizen first.

Nehru also created enduring civic institutions, a strong socially responsive judiciary, a commitment to national stewardship of the army and overall egalitarianism. His policies led to the setting up of India's infrastructure for scientific education, the nuclear and space programmes for peaceful use, the vast Indian Railways network, and the pharmaceutical industry.

What also made him a truly great democrat was his fairness and candour and he never abused authority. Needless to say, he diligently endeavoured to strengthen the autonomous nature and institutions of a newly independent India.

Nehru was arrested by the British and imprisoned for the first time in 1921. Over the next twenty four years, Nehru spent more than nine years in jail.

A wordsmith, Nehru was a prolific writer. He wrote most of his great works while in prison, most notable among them being 'Glimpses of World History' (1936), encompassing letters to his daughter, Indira Gandhi, and 'The Discovery of India (1946).'

Nehru's charisma was not confined to India alone. Much esteemed across the globe, Nehru gave India, an under–developed country, a great sense of respectability. It is a different matter that his legacy is now a 'Punching' bag for critics, because of his failure to adequately confront Pakistan and China when it was most needed (India's ignominious defeat in the war with China lowered Nehru's public stature, and only hastened his demise).

Nehru achieved so much more than most people can ever dream of in a lifetime, but like all great men, history has found him imperfect.

Bill Clinton

1946 –

Charismatic world leader

During the administration of William Jefferson Clinton, the U.S. enjoyed more peace and economic well being than at any time in its history. He was the first Democratic president since Franklin D. Roosevelt to win a second term. He could point to the lowest unemployment rate in modern times, the lowest inflation in 30 years, the highest home ownership in the country's history, dropping crime rates in many places, and reduced welfare roles. He proposed the first balanced budget in decades and achieved a budget surplus.

After the failure in his second year of a huge programme of health care reform, Clinton shifted emphasis, declaring 'The era of big government is over'. He sought legislation to upgrade education, to protect jobs of parents who must care for sick children, to restrict handgun sales, and to strengthen environmental rules.

President Clinton was born William Jefferson Blythe IV on August 19, 1946, in Hope, Arkansas, three months after his father died in a traffic accident. When he was four years old, his mother wed Roger Clinton, of Hot Springs, Arkansas. In high school, he took the family name.

He excelled as a student and as a saxophone player and once considered becoming a professional musician. As a delegate to Boys Nation while in high school, he met President John Kennedy in the White House Rose Garden. The encounter led him to enter a life of public service.

Clinton graduated from Georgetown University and in 1968 won a Rhodes Scholarship to Oxford University. He received a law degree from Yale University in 1973, and entered politics in Arkansas.

He was defeated in his campaign for Congress in Arkansas's Third District in 1974. The next year he married Hillary Rodham, a graduate of Wellesley College and Yale Law School. In 1980, Chelsea, their only child, was born.

Clinton was elected Arkansas Attorney General in 1976, and won the governorship in 1978. After losing a bid for a second term, he regained the office four years later, and served until he defeated incumbent George Bush and third party candidate Ross Perot in the 1992 presidential race.

Clinton and his running mate, Tennessee's Senator Albert Gore Jr., then 44, represented a new generation in American political leadership. For the first time in 12 years both the White House and Congress were held by the same party. But that political edge was brief; the Republicans won both houses of Congress in 1994. In 1998, as a result of issues surrounding personal indiscretions with a young woman White House intern, Clinton was the second U.S. president to be impeached by the House of Representatives. He was tried in the Senate and found not guilty of the charges brought against him. He apologised to the nation for his actions and continued to have unprecedented popular approval ratings for his job as president.

In the world, he successfully dispatched peace keeping forces to war–torn Bosnia and bombed Iraq when Saddam Hussein stopped United Nations inspections for evidence of nuclear, chemical, and biological weapons. He became a global proponent for an expanded NATO, more open international trade, and a worldwide campaign against drug trafficking. He drew huge crowds when he travelled through South America, Europe, Russia, Africa, and China, advocating U.S. style freedom.

Fidel Castro

1926 –

A great survivor

Fidel Castro, who comes from a wealthy Cuban farming family, was educated at Jesuit schools, and a preparatory school. He went to the University of Havana, in 1945, to study law and he graduated in 1950.

Castro practiced law for two years. Soon, he aimed to stand for parliament, but a coup led by General Fulgencio Batista toppled the government of Carlos Prío Socarrás. The elections were called off, and Castro was disappointed. He charged Batista for infringing on the constitution. His appeal was rejected. Irked considerably, Castro organised a fruitless armed attack in Oriente province. He was taken prisoner, tried, and sentenced to fifteen years in prison. He was released through an official pardon in 1955 and went into exile in Mexico and the U.S.

Castro set sail to Cuba, with other exiles who became known as the 26th of July Movement aboard a 60-ft pleasure craft in 1956. His outnumbered warriors got into action on December 2, 1956. While only a dozen of his men survived (this included Che Guevara, Raúl Castro, and Camilo Cienfuegos) and withdrew to engage in a guerrilla war against the Batista government, it was not long before Batista ordered over fifteen battalions to knock the stuffing out of them. However, Castro's dogged fighters managed to score a series of amazing victories. Batista's men were no match and forsook their loyalty. The writing was on the wall. Inevitably, Batista and president-elect Carlos Rivero Agüero took flight from Cuba on January 1, 1959. Castro was in control of Havana.

Castro got swift recognition from the U.S. However, when Cuba signed an agreement to buy oil from the Soviet Union, the U.S.–owned refineries in Cuba refused to process the oil. The U.S. also broke off diplomatic relations with the Cuban government. This led to a variety of pacts between Castro and the Soviets. As Soviet aid to Cuba began to pour in, the country also received large amounts of fiscal and military support.

In 1959, following President Dwight Eisenhower's ban on the import of Cuban sugar into the U.S., Castro nationalised $875 million worth of U.S. property and businesses. The U.S. now played with its sanctions, just as much as Castro has played tough with his own citizens. In 1961, the U.S. also made an unsuccessful attack on Cuba – quite (in)famously called the Bay of Pigs. The CIA's belief, that an invasion would spawn a popular uprising against Castro, was wrong. There was no such revolt.

An atheist, Castro went on the offensive. He affirmed that he was a Marxist–Leninist. He declared that Cuba would adopt Communism – the first socialist state to do so in the Western Hemisphere. The CIA continued its Sabotage–Castro operations; it could hardly do anything to unsettle the man, or his government. It is said that over 600 attempts to overthrow Castro have been made, all of them in vain.

The Soviets had once nursed the idea of placing missiles in Cuba. This was thought to be a deterrent to possible U.S. aggression against the island. The U.S. discovered the setting up of Soviet nuclear weapons, 150 km south of Miami, as a hostile act and a peril to U.S. security. This led to a crisis and the UN–implemented quarantine on Cuba. Castro

▶ A great survivor

now appealed to the Soviets to launch a nuclear first strike against the U.S., if Cuba was invaded. The Soviets did not acquiesce to his request. A compromise was, however, reached when the Soviets agreed to remove the missiles in a barter for U.S. commitment not to attack Cuba, and also freeze its missiles from Turkey.

Castro's pro-Soviet policy also led to a split between him and his fellow revolutionary Che Guevara, who had a China–centric orientation. When Che left for Bolivia to engineer a failed revolution against the country's military dictatorship, Castro did not commit any material support. He gave the excuse that the Soviets were not happy unless groups that followed their ideology were involved.

A truly great survivor, Castro has consolidated control of his nation by nationalising industry, filching property owned by Cubans/non–Cubans alike, and collectivising agriculture. However, he received a setback to his image when a bus of asylum seekers crashed through the gates of the Peruvian Embassy in Havana, in 1980. It is said that over 10,000 Cubans fled to the embassy within 2 days. Castro responded that anyone could leave the country by boat from Havana and as a result, nearly 125,000 Cubans took flight within a matter of days (Castro's daughter is also estranged, and now lives in the U.S.).

A failed leader, according to the U.S. government, Castro, in the twilight of his career, continues to hold on to power, somehow. The game goes on – without a winner in place.

Lord Carnarvon

1866 – 1923

The curse of the Mummy

George Edward Stanhope Molyneux Herbert, usually referred to simply as Lord Carnarvon, was the English aristocrat best known as the financier of the excavation of the Egyptian New Kingdom Pharaoh Tutankhamun's tomb in Egypt's Valley of the Kings.

Born at the family home Highclere Castle in Hampshire on June 26, 1866, George Herbert succeeded to the Carnarvon title in 1890. On June 26, 1895 Carnarvon married one Almina Victoria Maria Alexandra Wombwell, daughter of Marie Boyer, the wife of Frederick Charles Wombwell, but her real father was possibly the unmarried Rothschild family member Alfred Rothschild who made Lady Carnarvon his heiress. (Their grandson, Henry George Reginald Molyneux Herbert, 7th Earl of Carnarvon, was Racing Manager to Queen Elizabeth II from 1969, and one of Her Majesty's closest friends). Exceedingly wealthy, Lord Carnarvon was at first best–known as an owner of race horses and as a reckless driver of early automobiles, suffering a serious motoring accident in Germany in 1901 which left him significantly disabled.

The 5th Earl was an enthusiastic amateur Egyptologist, undertaking in 1907 to sponsor the excavation of the royal tombs at Thebes by Howard Carter. It was in 1922 that they together opened the tomb of Tutankhamun in the Valley of the Kings, exposing treasures unsurpassed in the history of archaeology. Several months later, Carnarvon died suddenly, giving popular credence to the story of the 'Curse of Tutankhamun', the 'Mummy's Curse' – his death is most probably explained by blood poisoning (progressing to pneumonia) after accidently shaving a mosquito bite infected with erysipelas. His colleague and employee, Howard Carter, he man most responsible for revealing the tomb of the young king, lived safely for another seventeen years.

Of the original team of archaeologists who were present when the ancient tomb of the boy king Tutankhamun was opened, only one lived to a ripe old age. Was this a bizarre coincidence? Or was it the manifestation of a curse that had passed down through the centuries?

The final wall of the sealed burial chamber of the boy pharaoh was breached for the first time in 3,000 years on 17 February 1923. Archaeologist Howard Carter whispered breathlessly that he could see 'Things, wonderful things' as he gazed in awe at the treasures of Tutankhamun. As Carter and Lord Carnarvon, looked at the treasures of gold, gems, precious stones and other priceless relics, they ignored the dire warning written all those centuries ago to ward off grave robbers. In the ancient hieroglyphics above their heads, it read: 'Death will come to those who disturb the sleep of the pharaohs.'

The final blow of the excavators' pick had set free the Curse of the Pharaoh. Lord Carnarvon had never taken lightly the threats of ancient Egypt's high priests. In England before his expedition had set out, he had consulted a famous mystic of the day, Count Hamon, who warned him that death will claim him in Egypt should he enter the tomb. The accolades of the world's academics rained down on Carnarvon and his team. The praise of museums and seats of learning as far apart as Cairo and California was heaped on them. Carnarvon revelled in the glittering prize of fame, little knowing that he had but two months to enjoy the fruits of his success. On 5 April 1923, just 47 days after breaching the chamber into Tutankhamun's resting place, Carnarvon died aged 57.

Jacques Cousteau

1910 - 1997

Captain of the oceans

Jacques-Yves Cousteau was a French naval officer, explorer and researcher who studied the sea and all forms of life in water. Cousteau was born in Saint André de Cubzac, France and died in Paris. Cousteau is generally known in France as le commandant Cousteau (Commander Cousteau).

In 1930 he was admitted to the École Navale (Naval Academy) in Brest and became a gunnery officer of the French Navy, which gave him the opportunity to make his first underwater experiments. He was training to become a pilot, but a serious car accident ended his aviation career. In 1936 he tested a model of underwater eyeglasses, perhaps the ancestors of modern masks.

Married in 1937 to Simone Melchior, he took part in World War II, and during the conflict he found the time to be co-inventor, with Emile Gagnan, of the first type of SCUBA diving equipment, the Aqua-Lung in 1943. Among the things that prompted him to develop efficient air-breathing free-swimming diving gear, were two oxygen toxicity accidents that he had earlier experienced with rebreathers.

In the post-WWII years, still a naval officer, he developed techniques for the minesweeping of France's harbors and explored shipwrecks. Named the president of the French Oceanographic Campaigns, in 1950 he bought his famous ship Calypso, with which he visited the most interesting waters of the planet, including some rivers. During these trips he produced many books and films. Cousteau won three Oscars for 'The Silent World', 'The Golden Fish' and 'World Without Sun', as well as many other top awards including the Palme d'Or in 1956 at the Cannes Film Festival. His work did a great deal to popularise knowledge of underwater biology.

In 1963 with Jean de Wouters, Cousteau developed the underwater camera named 'Calypso-Phot' which was later licensed to Nikon and became the 'Calypso-Nikkor' and then the 'Nikonos'.

Together with Jean Mollard he created the SP-350, a two-man submarine that could reach a depth of 350m below the ocean's surface. The successful experiment was soon repeated in 1965 with two submarines that reached 500m. Cousteau was made director of the Oceanographic Museum of Monaco, created the Underseas Research Group in Toulon, was the leader of the Conshelf Saturation Dive Programme (long-term immersion experiments, the first manned undersea colonies) and was one of the few foreigners that has been admitted to the American Academy of Sciences.

Cousteau's popularity was increasing. In October 1960, a large amount of radioactive waste was going to be discarded in the sea by EURATOM. Cousteau organised a publicity campaign which gained popular support. The train carrying the waste was stopped by women and children sitting on the railway, and was sent back to its origin. The risk was avoided.

In 1974 he created the Cousteau Society for the protection of ocean life, which now has more than 300,000 members.

In 1977, together with Peter Scott, he received the UN international environment prize, and a few years later he also received the American Liberty Medal from Jimmy Carter, then president of the U.S..

Now Cousteau's figure is admired, beloved worldwide through the many who love the sea, and is regarded with a sort of devotion, as symbolic of adventure, nature and exploration. Jacques Cousteau died on June 25, 1997, and is buried in the Cousteau family plot at Saint André de Cubzac, France.

David Suzuki

1936 –

The environment's prophet

David Takayoshi Suzuki was the broadcast journalist who popularised science in Canada and other parts of the world with untiring energy for more than three decades. Following a life trajectory similar to those of Carl Sagan, Jacques Cousteau and Stephen Hawking, Suzuki gravitated from pure research to presenting the mysteries of genetics, technology and environmental conservation in layman's terms. A passionate educator who maximised the potential of modern electronic media to reach out to millions of average viewers, Suzuki was one of the most respected and anticipated faces on television in North America.

For two generations of Canadians, Suzuki was a 'Great man' who did their cherished multiethnic heritage proud. Born to parents of Japanese origin in Vancouver who ran a dry cleaning store, he was introduced to the magic of nature by his father, who he described as 'My greatest inspiration and role model.' His earliest memories were of camping and fishing trips that instilled a green outdoors personhood.

After the Japanese attack on Pearl Harbour, Suzuki's family was rounded up by the Canadian government on grounds of suspicious loyalty. His father was deported to perform road labour while womenfolk and children were evacuated to interior British Columbia. Locked up in a decaying internment camp for three years, Suzuki had no school to attend but devised more enchanting learning sites– the lakes, rivers and mountains of the region. The young voyager defied laws forbidding internees to fish, playing cat–and–mouse with the authorities. He 'Learnt biology firsthand in the world, joyously and effortlessly.' Expelled to Ontario after World War II, Suzuki ventured on bicycling expeditions to understand birds, reptiles, insects and fish. Catch from these trips supplemented the family's hardship diet and adorned his amateur naturalist's home museum.

As a teenager, Suzuki was a loner. His aloofness was exacerbated by an overriding sense of inferiority imposed on Japanese Canadians. 'For an Asian to do as well as a white, he had to be ten times as good', he told an interviewer years later. As he grew older, a fierce desire to prove his worth motivated him. In the ninth grade he bagged an oratorical contest by regaling judges about animal adaptations.

In 1954, Suzuki was awarded a college scholarship to study in Massachusetts, U.S.A. Embryology and genetics courses brought out the best in him, 'My mouth hanging

▶ The environment's prophet

Previous page: David Suzuki popularised science in Canada and other parts of the world.
Opposite: Suzuki is a passionate educator who maximised the potential of modern electronic media to reach out to millions.

in astonishment at the beauty of the insights.' The ease with which he could explain highly technical concepts in lectures to fellow students and faculty members convinced him to discard medicine and pursue a career in research and teaching.

By 1961, Suzuki completed his Ph.D at the University of Chicago on chromosomal crossovers in fruit flies. His innate opposition to racial discrimination was strengthened in Tennessee, where he was a post–doctoral researcher, and where blacks were segregated. He identified with the sufferings of blacks, seeing 'my hang–ups about being Japanese in a white society as a mini–reflection of black problems.' He turned down job offers from three top American universities and returned to Canada.

From 1963, Suzuki embarked on an assistant professorship in genetics at the University of British Columbia, where his courses were so much in demand that the class had to be moved from a small room to a big hall. His laboratory research on mutations that could be controlled by temperature won the prestigious Steacie Memorial Fellowship. He also debuted as a broadcasting lecturer for community television programmes. Around 1970, while recording a show for the Canadian Broadcasting Corporation (CBC), he realised what a powerful medium TV was for 'making science available to the layperson.' Suzuki on Science, screened by CBC in 1971, attracted viewers to his passion for science and percipient interviews of fellow scientists.

Science Magazine and Quirks and Quarks (1974–1979) brought fame and mass adulation to Suzuki as the lovable anchor to radio listeners. These programmes were treasured as Canadian institutions. 'The Nature of Things' (1979 onward) was a show purchased by more stations outside Canada than any other CBC offering. In it, Suzuki unveiled the secrets of flora and fauna from an overt environmentalist angle. He strongly advocated limits on

human beings' reductive exploitation of nature. His philosophy was founded on the premise that mechanisation, technology and urbanisation severed human being's interconnectedness with nature. The sense of being an intimate part of nature was shattered, leading to loss of responsibility for actions.

Suzuki alerted against the potential of the misapplication of science for violence and warned that science was incapable of 'answering the most important questions– what is right and wrong, the differences between good and evil, the significance of murder or love.' In his autobiography, Metamorphosis, scientists were depicted as 'people with foibles.' Suzuki authored hundreds of articles and more than a dozen acclaimed books. In 1990, he was named Author of the Year in Canada. He received Canada's highest civilian honour and the United Nations Environment Programme Medal.

The David Suzuki Foundation was set up in 1990 with his second wife, a Harvard professor. It disseminated environmental consciousness and strategies for conservation to local communities. Suzuki's thinking on rights of Canada's aboriginal tribes intertwined forests and forest dwellers into one indivisible thread. He held up the example of indigenes to encourage a 'spiritual connection with nature' so that we consider water, air and soil our home. Illustrating Amazonian Indians and the Sans of the Kalahari Desert, he emphasised the importance of emotions and spirituality while conquering technological frontiers. Sensitive to concentration of knowledge in a power elite, he campaigned for bridging the digital divide in the information age.

A prophet who debunked the illusion that nothing lay beyond technology's reach, Suzuki urged the search for multiple truths via heterogeneous worldviews, utilising the magic wand of science.

Jonas Salk

1914 – 1995

A polio-free world

Jonas Salk was born in New York City of Russian–Jewish descent. His parents were not educated, but they were determined to make their children well–read and successful. Jonas was, indeed, the first member of his family to go to college. He went to the City College of New York aiming to first study law, but was soon spellbound by medicine and medical sciences.

When in medical school, Salk was asked to spend a year researching influenza. The dreaded virus that causes flu had just been discovered. The old scars of the flu epidemic that had devastated millions of lives at the beginning of World War I were fresh in everyone's memory, even though the development of vaccines in 1919 had stalled the spread of disease. Salk was keen to find out if the virus could be robbed of its facility to infect, while giving human subjects immunity from the illness. After intense study and experimentation, Salk succeeded. His toil had a dual effect. It also became the basis for his landmark work on polio.

In 1947, Salk accepted a position at the University of Pittsburgh Medical School. It was here that he saw the hope of developing a vaccine against polio. He dedicated himself to this task. His effort paid off eight years later. As human trials of the polio vaccine began in earnest, it vindicated Salk's dream – his vaccine had effectively protected subjects from the polio onslaught. When the discovery was announced in April 1955, Salk became a national hero.

A man with a big heart, Salk also won the affection of all when he refused to patent the vaccine. He had absolutely no intention to make money from his discovery. He wanted his vaccine to reach as many people as possible and to be available worldwide. He longed for a polio–free world.

What really made Salk's vaccine was the 'Killed' polio virus. The killed strain preserved the capability to immunise, but held no risk of infecting the subject. After a few years, a vaccine was made from live polio virus – one that could be administered orally, unlike Salk's vaccine which had to be injected. The oral option provided ease of use and no discomfort.

Salk's ground–breaking effort came from his application of findings he culled from many scientists. He not only found a way to produce large quantities of the virus, but also a method to kill them with formaldehyde, so that the virus remained intact enough to cause a reaction in human subjects. Salk first inoculated volunteers, including himself, his wife, and their three sons, in 1952, with a polio vaccine made from killed virus. All inoculated volunteers who took the test vaccine began producing antibodies to the disease. Astoundingly no one became ill. The vaccine seemed safe and effective.

Salk, the founder of the Salk Institute for Biological Sciences in La Jolla, California, who was truly one of the most highly thought of medical scientists of the Twentieth Century, published his results in 'The Journal of the American Medical Association,' the following year. This was followed by a nationwide testing of the vaccine. It was Salk's guru Thomas Francis Junior's brilliant vision that pictured mass vaccination of schoolchildren. The rest is now recorded history.

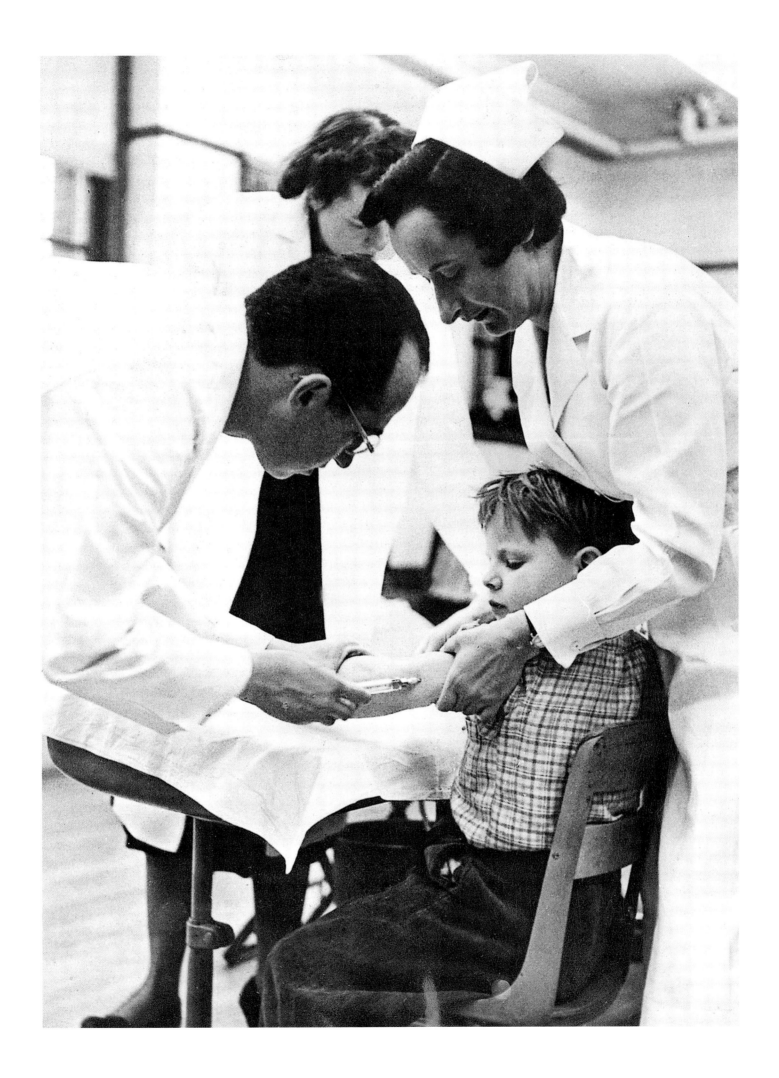

Christiaan Barnard

1922 - 2001

Transplant pioneer

One of the world's most ingenious surgeons, Christiaan Barnard was the son of a humble Afrikaner preacher and his wife. He grew up in Beaufort West. Barnard first studied medicine at the University of Cape Town, following which he completed his mandatory internship and residency at Groote Schuur Hospital in Cape Town. Subsequently, he became a general practitioner in Western Cape Province. In 1956, Barnard opted to enrol at the University of Minnesota to study surgery. And, while he was in Minneapolis he became fascinated in cardiology and cardiothoracic (heart–lung) surgery. He now preferred the subject to be his specialty. It was a momentous decision. It was to change the face of open heart surgery.

Barnard initiated the fascinating possibilities of open heart surgery, including several other ground–breaking surgical measures, at Groote Schuur Hospital (1958), where he was a senior cardiothoracic surgeon. Ever the experimenter and observer, Barnard first carried out a transplant on a human after he had meticulously researched the modus operandi on dogs.

Barnard established his first heart unit at Groote Schuur Hospital, and also lectured at the University of Cape Town. He became the head of the cardiothoracic surgery unit at the university, in 1961. A surgeon with intense alacrity, Barnard had also experimented for several years with animal heart transplants after having made his first success story with a successful kidney transplant (1954). Five years later, he became the earliest surgeon to perform the first–ever kidney transplant in South Africa. Barnard was also the first to show that intestinal atresia, a hereditary gap in the small intestine, is caused by deficient blood supply to the foetus during pregnancy.

Barnard made history on December 3, 1967, when he performed the first heart transplant ever. The patient was a fifty–five–year–old dentist, Louis Washkansky, who was ailing from both heart disease and diabetes. The heart came from a young woman, Denise Darvall, who had died in a road accident. It was a nine–hour long operation, manned by a team of 30. Washkansky made it through. He lived for eighteen days and succumbed to complications induced by immuno–suppressive drugs, which he was taking prior to surgery.

Barnard's second heart transplant was performed in January, the following year. The patient survived for just over a year and a half. His fifth and sixth patients survived thirteen and twenty four years, respectively.

Slowly, Barnard now began to work on and pioneer new and risky techniques. He laboured on and produced double transplants (1974) and artificial valves. He also used animal hearts for emergency treatment (1977). Between the years 1967-1973, Barnard performed 10 orthotopic transplants; he went on to conduct fourty eight heterotopic transplants between 1975 and 1983. The introduction of the drug, cyclosporine was god–sent, at this point of time. It stabilised and regulated orthotopic operations. As honours showered one after the other, Barnard continued his work vigorously, earning dozens of success stories along the way.

Celebrated around the world for his enterprising achievement, Barnard was troubled by rheumatoid arthritis since childhood. When the problem started troubling his magical hands, with severity, he decided to give up surgery (1983). Following his retirement, Barnard settled down comfortably at his ranch in South Africa. A heart transplant pioneer par excellence, Barnard died due an acute asthma attack, while on a vacation in Cyprus in 2001.

William Boeing

1881 - 1956

Power of innovation

Among the pioneers who transformed the world with the powers of innovation, daring and enterprise, William Edward Boeing stands tall. He was the personification of avant–garde ideas and the unique American sense of imagination that soared to dazzling heights, literally. The father of commercial aviation who dreamt of alternative means of commuting to ships and railways, Boeing set into motion a process that shrunk the world and made it faster and easier to travel.

Born to an educated and wealthy timber baron of German origin, Boeing was christened 'Wilhelm'. A happy childhood in Detroit, Michigan State, was interrupted at the age of eight when his father died and he was sent to Switzerland for part of his education. He enrolled in Sheffield Scientific School at Yale University from 1899 to 1902 for the engineering degree, but quit before graduating with the intention of 'Doing something on my own.'

Moving to the Pacific Northwest, Boeing set up his own timber business and prospered like his father on the Washington State coast. In 1910, he attended the first American Air Meet in Los Angeles and was captivated by the concept of flying. He tried to get a test ride but failed. Boeing used to frequent the Seattle University Club, where he struck a thick friendship with a Naval engineer obsessed with flight. In 1914, the two men bought rides in a rickety seaplane and began planning improvements in the craft. In 1915, Boeing travelled to southern California for flight instructions at the Glenn Martin Flying School and bought a seaplane, a novelty in those days. He was an avid fisher-man and wanted a fast means of transportation between his Seattle home and his favourite angling waters, the Canadian lakes. The Martin hydroplane nearly killed him on the flight home, as it sheared off pontoons while landing. Hearing that it would take months before spare parts could be sent from LA, Boeing and his engineer friend began to redesign the entire plane.

Convinced that the future lay in aviation, Boeing founded the Pacific Aero Products Company in 1916 and constructed the B&W seaplane using piano wire, spruce lumber and strong linen fabric. When the first test flight was scheduled and the pilot ended up inexplicably late, Boeing climbed into the cockpit and flew the plane himself, explaining later that he 'Did not want to endanger anyone else.' A dashing entrepreneur, he was aware of the risks he was taking with the firm conviction possessed by people normally destined for a place in history.

During World War I, Boeing served as a lieutenant in the U.S. Navy. A shrewd businessman, Boeing claimed that people were not taking the war seriously enough, jumped in a plane and dropped leaflets all over Seattle, advertising military preparedness. When the time came, the patriotic Boeing was awarded a very lucrative contract by the military to build training, observatory, attack, and pursuit planes. The renamed eponymous Boeing Airplane Company supplied crafts to the U.S. armed forces for the next 15 years.

After 1918, Boeing tried to persuade the federal government not to release surplus planes into the commercial market fearing competition. When that move failed, he briefly returned to the furniture and speedboat business. During the slump period in the airplane market, he depleted his personal fortune to keep company workers employed, another sign that Boeing was playing for the long haul.

In 1925, the U.S. government opened postal services to private operators. Boeing won the contract to fly mail between Chicago and San Francisco with his fleet of Model 40As– each containing a tiny compartment for passengers. 'From the start of the mail operation,' he declared, 'I looked ahead to the time when passengers would become of primary importance.' Passenger service evolved out of Boeing's airmail service and caught on like wildfire in late 1920s America.

Boeing set up a holding company that included airplane manufacturing, airmail contracts and a passenger service known as United Aircraft & Transport Corporation. He also opened a School of Aeronautics in Oakland to raise standards of flying and provide United Air Lines with capable pilots. In 1933, The Boeing Company introduced the world's first modern passenger transport, the Model 247.

Boeing indulged in stock manipulations and pyramiding for his holding company and reached an incredible million percent market capitalisation before the Great Depression. He manoeuvred many corporate buyouts and takeovers and built a formidable monopolistic conglomerate. Navy and army shopping orders for Boeing remained consistently high until 1933. His rivalry with Donald Douglas was one of the most intense corporate clashes in American capitalism. In 1934, federal antitrust laws forbade airmail carriers from associating with aircraft manufacturers. Boeing's empire was forced to split back into separate companies. The government cancelled airmail contracts with private planes. Boeing, the subject of a Senate investigation for amassing stratospheric wealth, was the only one who didn't get his contracts back. Angered by the probe and the losses, he quit in disgust, sold all his aviation stocks at the age of 52 and exited the industry.

Boeing retired but left a skilled management team in place that took the company to the pinnacle of American technological leadership. The company retained his legendary 'Anything is possible' credo and went from strength to strength, overcoming insuperable hurdles in tight situations. A reserved man who zealously guarded his privacy, Boeing was feted with the Guggenheim medal in 1934 for his contribution to avionics. In 1954, two years before his death, he was the guest of honour at the ceremonies marking the introduction of the Boeing 707, America's first commercial jet airplane.

Boeing was alacritous to pounce on opportunities and perspicacious to cut loose and divest when the going went nowhere. His chequered fortunes illustrated the importance of government patronage in an era when flight was viewed primarily from military security lenses. However, the most significant upshot of his foresight and self–belief was the universalisation of civil aviation.

Opposite: William Boeing (right) and pilot Eddie Hubbard carried the first U.S. international airmail in this Boeing Model C from Vancouver, Canada to Seattle, Washington.

Wright brothers

1913 – 1980

Aviation pioneers

Orville Wright (1871–1948), and Wilbur Wright (1867–1912), American airplane inventors and aviation pioneers, the sons of a pastor showed a restive fondness for mechanics from childhood. Academics did not quite appeal to them and they never contemplated graduation. This was the key element that helped them open a bicycle sales and repair shop in Dayton, Ohio.

Great entrepreneurs and brilliant mechanics, the Wrights were soon manufacturing their own bicycles and selling them. The urge to read about new experiments was quite remarkably their staple food. When they came across news stories of the German engineer Otto Lilienthal's fatal glider flight, they lost no time in building their own in 1899, a biplane kite with mechanical wings. Within a year's time, they also began their experiments on their new handiwork, and went to Kitty Hawk, North Carolina, to fine–tune, because they felt that the sand hills provided the best open air laboratory to conduct their glider experiments.

They also built the first wind tunnel. In the process, they launched their own tables of lift–pressures for various wing surfaces and wind speeds resulting in a new powered acquisition, the powerful four–cylinder engine, and a propeller. Back they went to Kitty Hawk, but the weather stayed away. They had to wait until December 17, 1903, when Orville piloted a flight of 12 seconds, at 120 feet. Wilbur extended the flight time. He stayed afloat for 59 seconds and covered 852 feet. History was made.

The Wrights' first airplane was built at a cost of approximately $1,000, with wings 12 meters long; it weighed 340 kilograms with the pilot. The Wright brothers used their own bicycle facility for the construction of their early aircraft admirably. They moved portions of the wing assembly,

not shifts in bodily weight. This was a landmark advance that augmented the aircraft's position in flight and design. When Orwell designed an engine, and fixed it on their improved glider, it was a small step in history, and a giant leap in air for mankind.

This pumped up their adrenaline and the crusade for innovation. They worked on a more efficient and reliable prototype and came up with two powerful planes over the next two years and quickly procured a U.S. patent for powered aircraft in 1906. They also sold their plane to the British and French governments; however, two years later, the U.S. War Department contracted the Wrights for their flying machine for the army.

In 1909, they launched the American Wright Company and started manufacturing superior planes. The Wright brothers, both bachelors, quickly became household names worldwide. They had just one focus – to perfect their airplane and, make it better at every step. They had great foresight and vision. They not only hoped that airplanes would be used to carry passengers and mail, but also help prevent war.

In the midst of all adulation, Wilbur, died of typhoid, in May 1912. Three years later, Orville, who, of course, never gave up test flying, bid adieu from the aircraft manufacturing business. He got into aviation research full–time, and when World War I erupted, he accepted a commission as a Major. He served as a consultant for the air service, and continued to be on the Board of National Advisory Committee for Aeronautics for several years after the Great War ended.

What's most amazing about the Wrights' first craft was its basic principles of aviation – now still being used in every aeroplane.

Albert Einstein

1879 – 1955

A passion for knowledge

Albert Einstein, the greatest of theoretical physicists, was born in Germany. His father owned a small electrochemical industrial unit. Albert attended a Catholic elementary school, because his parents were not rigidly Jewish and at the behest of his mother, he was driven into music.

When his father first showed him a receptacle compass, it was like what the falling apple was to his illustrious scientific forebear, Sir Isaac Newton. Einstein was barely five years old, but he felt an indescribable experience. His mind lit up in an epiphany, and he began his long adventure in science.

Ironically, Einstein, despite his passion for knowing, was thought to be a slow learner by his peers. He built models and mechanical gadgets for joy but psychologists who deciphered his consciousness, when he had grown to be a legend, felt that Albert, as a child, suffered from dyslexia. This was further strengthened by observations that his plain shyness sprung from the notably unusual structure of his brain, which was scientifically examined after his death.

Einstein, researchers also suggest, was able to turn science inside-out, thanks to his non–obsessive attitude with space and time. This, they further observe, led him on his great path for the development of the theory of relativity – his most celebrated discovery. It is also said that his unhurried thought process laid the foundation to his science, unlike most children who find no time for mental fine–tuning. Further, and as with all great men, who come under the scanner long after they are gone, Einstein, studies suggest, may have also had Asperger's syndrome – a disorder related to autism.

Einstein began to dabble in mathematics when he was hardly twelve, although it's whispered that he had failed in the subject as he progressed with his academic pursuits. It's a fact that Einstein was encouraged to study science and mathematics by his uncles seemed to have made them happy, if not proud, with his skills.

Einstein, because he had a mind of his own, did not relish the harsh regulation of German schools. He was not an exceptional student, but what he liked best was doing his own thing. That he loved philosophy, mathematics, and science, is beyond an iota of doubt. What is not widely known is he was his own apprentice in them and not quite keen to learn them in school.

When Einstein's parents moved to Italy in 1895, as his father's business could no longer sustain them, Albert

▶ A passion for knowledge

Previous page: Einstein once said 'If A is a success in life, then A equals x plus y plus z. Work is x; y is play; and z is keeping your mouth shut.'
Opposite: When Einstein won the Nobel Prize in 1921 for his photoelectric law and work in the field of theoretical physics, there was no mention of the word, relativity.

was left behind to continue with his studies. Einstein, who never fancied toughlearning, left school without a certificate, and rejoined his family. He now immersed himself into his own private studies. It was at this time that he learned calculus and some of the more complex principles of science. Curiously, Einstein failed in his entrance test for admission to the famed Swiss Federal Institute of Technology in Zurich. He was quite desolate. However, he gained entry to the Institute and graduated in physics and mathematics in 1900.

Einstein became a Swiss citizen, the following year. He was also hired as a technical assistant at the Swiss Patent Office. Two years later, he married his original flame, Mileva Maric. The patent office was Einstein's grand laboratory; his radar and compass in theoretical physics. By 1905, he had published an article titled 'A New Determination of Molecular Dimensions' in 'Annalen der Physik,' a physics magazine of repute. The submission fetched him a Ph.D., from the University of Zurich. Buoyant with the progression, Einstein published four more papers in 'Annalen'. This included his ground–breaking theory that light exists in both waves and particles. His paper shelved the conventional view that time and space were absolute concepts; it also deliberated that both time and space differ with circumstances.This sent the scientific world into a flurry.

Einstein had now moved places in the scientific sense. He not only opted for the position of Professor of Physics in Prague and Zurich University, but also moved from there to Berlin with his wife and two sons (1914). The Prussian Academy of Sciences was his next destination. Strangely enough, he was not innately happy in Berlin; hence, he returned with his family to Switzerland just before World War I. The Einsteins separated at the end of the Great War, and Albert married his second cousin, Elsa Lowenthal, the following year (1919).

In the midst of change, Einstein had perfected his general theory of relativity (1915). He emerged with his famous mathematical equation $E=mc^2$ (energy equals mass times the speed of light squared). His theory of relativity also appeared in print. 'The Principle of Relativity, Sidelights on Relativity,' and 'The Meaning of Relativity' (1919). The Royal Society of London noted that the solar eclipse, that took place the same year, had confirmed Einstein's general theory of relativity. Einstein was now the toast of the entire world. As his fame spread far and wide, Albert, like all great men, was not exempt from criticism, by his peers on the groundwork of his political ideologies. In the years that followed, he began to be as much disliked for his scientific theory, just as much as he was appreciated for his vigorous stand on peace, liberty and justice.

When Einstein won the Nobel Prize in 1921 for his photoelectric law and work in the field of theoretical physics, there was no mention of the word, relativity, his landmark breakthrough. What a paradox! Undaunted, Einstein continued to work just as passionately, trying to coalesce his concept of gravity and electromagnetism into a 'Grand unified theory of physics.' In other words a single mathematical formula that could amalgamate the universal properties of matter and energy. It's a voyage that Einstein was sadly unable to complete.

Einstein foresaw the Nazi spectre; he saw the employment of the atom bomb with as much distress. And, yet, he never ever shirked his stand for pacifism to make our world a better place to live in.

Einstein once mused; 'The most beautiful thing we can experience is the mysterious. It is the source of all true art and all science. He to whom this emotion is a stranger, who can no longer pause to wonder and stand rapt in awe, is as good as dead: his eyes are closed.'

Sigmund Freud

1856 – 1939

Comprehension of the mind

Sigmund Freud was born in Freiberg, Moravia. However, not much is known of his early life as he twice burned his personal papers. Besides, his later papers were strictly 'Embargoed' in the Sigmund Freud Archives; some were only made available to Ernest Jones, his official biographer, and also select members of the interior loop of psychoanalysis.

Freud was a bright student and a child with endless curiosity. He went to the medical school, and graduated with relative ease. However, side–by–side with his learning, Freud had a fondness for the unexplained. He dwelled on his own eclectic research activity, which may not have appealed to the purists. He came under the influence of the famous neurologist, Jean Charcot and, the rest was destiny. He learned hypnosis under Charcot, an interest he was to give up later. His daughter, Anna, a noted psychologist, followed in his footsteps with finesse.

Freud first set up his practice in Vienna, and it was here that he spent his formative years in exploring the human mind, an activity that was to make him famous. He first used the term psychoanalysis in 1896.

Freud developed a theory of the human mind and human behaviour, and clinical techniques for attempting to help irrational (neurotic) patients. Most experts today claim to have been enthused by one, not the other. However, the most significant contribution Freud has made to modern thought is his idea of the unconscious. His model of the unconscious was groundbreaking, in a world dominated by positivism. Freud proposed that awareness existed in layers and there were thoughts occurring 'Below the surface.' Dreams, he explained was the 'Royal road to the unconscious.' In his seminal work, 'The Interpretation of Dreams' (1900), Freud developed the argument that the unconscious exists, and described a method for acquiring admission to its deepest recesses.

It was, however, his psychoanalytic structure, 'Three Essays on the Theory of Sexuality' (1905), that alienated him from the mainstream of contemporary psychiatry, and also his two loyal disciples, Alfred Adler and Carl Jung. Adler went on to develop his own psychology, which emphasised the belligerence with which people are deficient in some quality (inferiority complex) and convey their unhappiness by 'Staging.' Freud did not lament losing Adler nor Jung. Freud and Jung were close for several years, but Jung's aspirations, and his emergent liking for religion and mysticism pushed them apart. Freud, the Wizard of Dreams, went on with his oeuvre, liked or not

▶ Comprehension of the mind

Previous page and opposite: Freud developed a theory of the human mind and human behaviour, and clinical techniques for attempting to help irrational (neurotic) patients. Most experts today maintain to have been enthused by one, not the other.

liked. He thought of society as composed of rules from within. Of rules meant to subdue the tides of emotional excess that surge too freely within. He also believed that contentment arises from attuning one's life with one's true feelings.

A plumber of the unconscious, Freud not only focused on the vitality of self–awareness as being fundamental to psychological insight, but he also thought of the emotional brain as being full of symbolic meaning: the interaction of metaphors, stories, myths, and the arts. Freud believed that dreams also represent the unconscious trying to express itself consciously.

Interestingly, Freud's antipathy towards religion was, in more ways than one, legendary, albeit he often referred to the experience of nirvana as the 'Awful depths' of Eastern thought in metrical terms. His perspective, arguably, leaves too little space for descriptions that show the positive contributions of spirituality in child development. What's more, new research has clearly demonstrated children's capacity for profound religious thought. But, this does not digress from Freud's major contribution to his celebrated theory of conscience: of how it is formed out of primitive fears, which is also contiguous with his brilliant analyses of the human instinct, and the concept of character or the self from infancy to maturity.

What makes Freud's work unique is the reader finds himself/herself in the world of dreams. Of the existence of dreams for the importance and sense of it, including the elements of wish-fulfilment brought through an objective of realisation, or reduplication, of what Freud called dream work. In its totality, Freud's study of dreams also led him directly into the practical applications of psychoanalysis as a tool for neuroses. It elevated his acumen to unlock the difficulties and perplexities of the hidden side of human nature – a clear path into what makes the unconscious mental life a subject to the action of the mechanisms which are not explicable by the means at hand, or ordinary rationalised thinking. His expansive experiments balanced the domain that went beyond all negations with the unconscious. It also set the ball rolling, while beginning to read Freud's own emerging conception of the psyche into a more elementary, psychological trepidation.

With his introduction of the id, the superego, and their problem–child, the ego, Freud also advanced scientific comprehension of the mind infinitely. In so doing, he ripped open motivations that are normally imperceptible to our consciousness. While there's no question that his own prejudices and neuroses influenced his observations, the components are less consequential than his paradigm shift as a whole. That he went overboard with some of his theories, and manipulated them, is part of history.

With today's technology, the efficacy of Freudian analysis remains a topic of disagreement, though the likelihood of integrating psychoanalysis and drug therapy is gaining some ground.

Freud 'Meditated' upon others' minds as much as he did his own. He believed it was conceivable to lay bare the content of the unconscious if one paid attention to such normal behaviours as jokes, slips of the tongue, free associations and most importantly, dreams. Convinced of its import, Freud is also reported to have quipped that a marble tablet, on his home, would one day read: 'Here, on July 24, 1895, the secret of the dream revealed itself to Dr Sigmund Freud.'

If dreams are made this way, Freud made his own. He peered deeply into his own psyche, and into that of all human beings.

Edwin Hubble

1889 – 1953

A fascination with science

The great astronomer and scientist Edwin Hubble was born in Marshfield, Missouri on November 20th 1889. He attended high school when his family migrated to Chicago.

Hubble was fascinated with science and exploring new worlds from his childhood. An avid reader and fan of Jules Verne and Henry Rider Haggard's fascinating books, Hubble was also a committed student. He excelled in sports and managed to pursue his studies with just as much enthusiasm as winning medals in his sporting quests.

After having majored as an undergraduate in science at the University of Chicago, Hubble went to Oxford on a Rhodes scholarship. He did not give up his sports philosophy in the midst of academics. His physique was strong; his mind just as spirited. He was handsome too, and his charm fluttered many a heart. It was only when his dying father insisted that he should study law rather than science that Hubble changed his track. Curiously, he also began to study literature and Spanish. On his return to the U.S., Hubble took up the position of a Spanish teacher in a high school. However, his longing for science never abandoned him – it had only strengthened.

Hubble's passion for science led him to sign on as a graduate student at Yerkes Observatory in Wisconsin. It was just what the doctor had ordered. He began to work fervently in his study of pale, misty dots of light called nebulae or cloud.

In 1917, Hubble received a doctorate in astronomy from the University of Chicago. He joined the respected Mount Wilson Observatory. Earlier, the call of duty had taken him to World War I. But, once the war was over, Hubble arrived at the observatory headquarters, still in his army Major's uniform. He took off quickly from where he had left and began examining the universe with the newly arrived 100–inch Hooker Telescope, the most powerful instrument at the time.

In 1924, Hubble established the fact that there were galaxies other than the Milky Way. Five years later, he demonstrated that the galaxies were receding from Earth. A landmark discovery that proved that the universe was still expanding. The observation led Hubble to establish the numerical relationship between a galaxy's distance and the speed of recession. It was given the name Hubble's constant.

As a result of it and other findings, Hubble's work laid a new foundation in the study of cosmology. By the end of the 1940s, he had become a huge icon.

▶ A fascination with science

Previous page: Hubble had absolutely no trouble in acquiring a giant telescope at Mount Wilson. Opposite: the Hubble Space Telescope, which was deployed in space in 1990, was named after him.

He now shifted his devotion to the newly constructed 200–inch telescope on Mt. Palomar, an abode which remained his temple of study until his death. No small wonder why the Hubble Space Telescope, which was deployed in space in 1990, was named after him.

Hubble, the winner of the Bruce Medal and the Gold Medal of the Royal Astronomical Society, also discovered the Asteroid 1373 Cincinnati and the Asteroid 2069 Hubble, which is rightly named after him. This was not all. Hubble has been credited to have solved four of the central difficulties in cosmology. His proposed classification system for nebulae, both galactic (diffuse) and extragalactic, has been one of them. This classification system for the galaxy has been christened as the Hubble morphological sequence of galaxy types. His discovery of Cepheids in NGC 6822 and analogous work in M33 and M31 have also established with certainty the nature of the galaxies. Hubble's work has also proved that the galaxies truly mark a space significant to the universe itself. Hubble also established the linear velocity–distance relation that verified and extended the relation to large redshifts (the frequency of a photon towards lower energy, or longer wavelength). This discovery holds the key to the notion of the expanding universe which is fundamental to cosmological models today.

Hubble's work also determines the existence of several other galaxies such as our own Milky Way, which was earlier believed to be the universe. He also devised a classification system for the various galaxies and sorted them by content, distance, shape, and brightness. He noticed redshifts in the emission of light from the galaxies. He saw they were moving away from each other at a rate constant to the distance between them. As a result, he formulated Hubble's Law – a principle that helped astronomers establish the age of the universe, and also prove that it is expanding.

Hubble's observations have revolutionised astronomy. It not only helped us realise there were other galaxies in the universe besides our own, but it also helped astronomers verify that if the universe was expanding outwards, it must have been coming from a central point, and that something must have caused that expansion to begin with – the origin of the famed Theory of the 'Big Bang'.

When World War II broke out, Hubble had the desire to enlist in the army and offered to work as a scientist. Following the defeat of Nazi Germany, Hubble was awarded the Medal of Merit and also elected Honourary Fellow of Queen's College, Oxford, for his matchless contribution to astronomy.

Hubble had absolutely no trouble in acquiring a giant telescope as soon as he got back to Mount Wilson so that he and his dedicated protégé could further explore the universe outside our galaxy. He did not stop at that. He followed it up by designing and setting up the colossal Hale Telescope, at the Mount Palomar Observatory.

Needless to say, Hubble had the single honour of being the first to use it. When a journalist asked him what he hoped to find with the new telescope, Hubble is reported to have quipped: 'We hope to find something we hadn't expected.' This was the real secret of his pioneering mind.

Hubble was truly a man of science. He will be forever remembered as the father of observational cosmology and the stars of the wide universe.

Henry Ford

1863 – 1947

An entrepreneur beyond compare

Born into a wealthy Michigan farming family, Henry Ford was the eldest of six children. From his childhood, Ford had a penchant for mechanics. Even before he reached his teens he indulged in his obsession at a mechanic's shop. His world lit up when he first chanced his ingenious eye on an internal combustion engine.

Ford first went to Detroit to work as a trainee machinist. Soon after his apprenticeship, he joined the Westinghouse Company working on gasoline engines. He married Clara Bryant in 1888. When he took up the position of an engineer with the Edison Illuminating Company (1891), which was soon followed by his promotion to Chief Engineer, Ford plunged himself into personal experiments on his great fascination, the internal combustion engine.

In 1896, he developed a self–propelled vehicle, which he christened the 'Quadricycle'. He test–drove his machine day and night until fully satisfied. This was his first automobile; the first that he handled from the driver's seat. Ford soon gave up his post at Edison. He was joined by a group of investors who shared his vision. This resulted in the emergence of the Detroit Automobile Company. The company ran into trouble because Ford was too preoccupied with design and not selling automobiles. Not that he

was a failure. On the contrary, he raced his car to victories and proved the superior character of his design. Notwithstanding the success, Ford had to quit the company. The company was, thereafter, restructured and became known as Cadillac.

Ford was an irrepressible champion of his own destiny. Unfazed, he along with eleven other investors with $28,000 as capital in the kitty now formed the Ford Motor Company (1903). Now a newly–designed car, Ford's model began with a bang and achieved a new land speed record. Barney Oldfield, a great driver of his time, was delighted with the machine. He took the car across the country. In the early 1900s, Ford released the Model T.

By the end of World War I (1918), almost 50 per cent of cars on American roads were Model T's. By 1927, Ford had produced from its assembly–line fifteen million Model T cars, an automobile record that stood on its own for the next half–century. Thereafter, its magic began to fade. Ford was a stickler for work ethics. He expected his workers to put their hearts out to the company. He paid them well, far beyond accepted wages of the time. He never liked labour unions; it was not until an agitation at United Auto Workers Union (1941), that a semblance of a union emerged at Ford.

▶ An entrepreneur beyond compare

Previous page: Ford was an irrepressible champion of his own destiny. He along with eleven other investors, with $28,000 as capital, formed the Ford Motor Company in 1903.
Opposite: In 1896, Ford developed a self–propelled vehicle, which he christened the Quadricycle. He test–drove his machine day and night until fully satisfied.

Ford's attempt for a seat in the U.S. Senate (1919) was a disappointment. He now handed over the presidency of his company to his son, Edsel. However, he continued to maintain a firm grip on management decisions and policies. It was only in 1956 that the company became partly–public, and not a fully–owned family business.

Ford's adamant mindset did not, at first, accept the decline in the Model T's fortune. He only relented because a new model was needed to fuel the balance sheet of the company, more so if it wanted to sustain itself. Edsel impressed upon his father that the need for change was a necessity. The company now made a new policy decision there would be a model change system in the company every year. It's a rule that is followed by most auto–making companies today.

Besides his love for cars, Ford, an entrepreneur beyond compare, had several other interests – he was a master of finance, he knew the potential of plastics. He used them in Ford automobiles throughout the 1930s. He also patented a light–weight automobile, made entirely of plastic. It ran on grain alcohol, or ethanol alcohol fuel, instead of gasoline.

Ford was also an avid fan of 'Americana'. He loved American folk music, square dancing, and also sponsored them. An early champion–sponsor of aviation, Ford also built the Dearborn Inn, the first airport hotel. He, with Edsel, also founded the Ford Foundation (1936), as a local (Michigan) philanthropy with a broad charter to promote human welfare. The Foundation, no longer associated with Ford Company or its family, is today both national and international in scope.

Edsel's death (1943) came as a big blow to Ford. It created a vacuum in the company. Edsel's widow Eleanor, who had naturally inherited her late husband's voting stocks, wanted their son Henry Ford II, to fill the position. Ford, now 79, took over the presidency. The issue was resolved.

This was also a difficult time. The company went through a bad patch and lost $10 million a month. President Franklin Roosevelt ratified federal aid for Ford Motor Company to continue war–time production of cars.

Ford also had a special affection for the newspaper, The 'Dearborn Independent', which he bought in 1919. The paper was labelled as 'Anti–immigrant, anti–labour, anti–liquor and anti–Semitic,' by critics. It ran for eight years. Ford also published in his name several anti–Jewish articles for the paper. It is said, with some plausible evidence, that Ford financed Adolf Hitler and his Nazi Party in their early political endeavours. This was not all. Ford also opened an assembly plant in Berlin in 1938 and supplied trucks to the Wehrmacht.

Ford was awarded the Grand Cross of the Order of the German Eagle (Großkreuz des Deutschen Adlerordens). He was the first American, and the fourth individual, decorated with Nazi Germany's highest honourary award for foreigners. The award cited that Ford was the recipient of the honour 'In recognition of [Ford's] pioneering effort in making motor cars available for the masses.' The award also carried a private laudatory note from Hitler. This gave him a dubious name. A pioneer, Ford died of a cerebral haemorrhage at age 83.

Osama bin Laden

1957 –

The world's most wanted fugitive

Osama bin Muhammad bin Laden was the man who single-handedly polarised public opinion with horrifying acts of violence, prompting scholars to brand him the causative for 'World War III'. An arch terrorist mastermind to some and a heroic freedom fighter to others, he rejuvenated Islamic extremism to take on the mightiest of powers. His life vindicated the truism that charismatic individuals influenced the course of history.

Born in Riyadh to a prosperous Yemeni immigrant clan close to the Saudi royal family, bin Laden grew up in an ambience of piety and opulence. Like other Arabic scions, he travelled to Beirut for studies between 1968 and 1970. Contrary to rumours, he was believed to be devout, self-effacing and attached to Islamic values in his teens, completing traditional education in a Jeddah high school.

In 1975, bin Laden entered King Abdelaziz University and married a Syrian relative. In time, he took at least three other wives and fathered 23 or more children. His outlook towards women and family was Quranic, dovetailing an obsession with Islam's lost masculinity. After graduating with a civil engineering degree, he joined the bin Laden business empire in an upper management position and cemented ties with the Saudi monarchy. Prince

Turki Faisal, the country's intelligence chief, trusted his organisational skills enough to award him command of a massive recruitment drive for Arab mujahideen (soldiers of God) being sent to evict the Soviets from Afghanistan.

In 1980, eager to demonstrate valour and defend Afghanistan's Muslims, bin Laden shifted base to the Pakistani border town of Peshawar. The anti–Soviet jihad gave him the perfect platform for displaying personal bravery. He engaged in personal hand-to-hand combat with the Red Army in Jaji and Shaban and earned his stripes as a true mujahid by getting injured in battle. He built tunnels, mosques, schools, clinics and refugee shelters, winning accolades from the local communities that hosted him.

He perfected the tactics of mixing charity and humanitarian work with militancy to good effect. For admiring Afghans, he appeared a prince who sacrificed his riches and comforts for the sake of defending Islam. One guerrilla remarked: 'He not only gave money to the cause, he gave the gift of himself.'

Around 1985, realising the international implications of the anti–Soviet jihad, bin Laden began networking with radical Islamists across the board. A phenomenal galvaniser of men and materials, he converted the Afghan

► The world's most wanted fugitive

Previous page and Opposite: So manic was bin Laden's assault that the U.S. launched two wars in his name in 2001 (Afghanistan) and 2003 (Iraq). A $25 million reward notwithstanding, he evaded the American dragnet and released chilling tape–recorded and video messages to the media, urging fresh uprisings against the U.S. and its allies.

resistance group Maktab-al-Khidmat into a global Islamic Rapid Reaction Force called Al Qaeda. In 1989, he arranged for the assassination of his own teacher, the Maktab's Palestinian leader, who opposed ramification of the struggle into a universal one. It was a sign of his utter ruthlessness towards opponents.

Al Qaeda was founded on bin Laden's Salafi ideals that spurned sectarian schisms and united Shiites and Sunnis against common enemies. From the early 1990s, he invited Islamists of varied strands to join Al Qaeda's council, laying the spadework for a gargantuan infrastructure that spawned cells in over 100 countries. The quality of recruits being of paramount importance, he accepted only 3,000 (3 percent) of the mujahideen who trained in Afghanistan and Pakistan between 1989 and 2001, screening out all but the most committed, trustworthy and capable fighters. This exclusivity made him legendary and enviable in the eyes of Islamic fundamentalists around the planet. Al Qaeda was structured so that it could survive without a single operational headquarters. Employing encrypted websites, satellite telephones, laptops and propaganda tools, he oversaw this decentralised organisation from multiple locations.

In 1990, bin Laden publicly fell out with his former benefactors in the Saudi government over halting aid to the mujahideen once the Soviets withdrew from Afghanistan. A seminal event that confirmed his dissidence was Iraq's invasion of Kuwait. Bin Laden petitioned his government to allow the formation of a mujahideen army to halt Saddam Hussein. Instead, when Riyadh allied with the U.S. and allowed American troops to set foot in Islam's holy lands, bin Laden was infuriated. The longer Christian soldiers stayed on in Saudi Arabia, the more radical his plans turned.

In 1991, bin Laden relocated to Sudan to escape the Saudi government's snare. He forged strong friendships with Sudanese Islamists and diversified his businesses by establishing thirty companies ranging from genetic research labs to construction. He even bailed out the Sudanese government with a $50 million bank deposit. Profits were ploughed back to expand Al Qaeda into a dreaded elite force capable of carrying out daredevil missions.

Embarrassed by international pressure on Al Qaeda, Sudan requested that bin Laden depart the country in 1996. He returned to Afghanistan–Pakistan, befriending the fundamentalist Taliban. Here, he engineered a tactical shift from concentrating mainly on puppet Muslim rulers of Egypt and Saudi Arabia to a 'Second front' against the 'King of Satan', America. In 1998, he announced the formation of 'World Islamic Front for Jihad Against Jews and Crusaders.' His new fatwa, ordering Muslims to kill Americans, did not distinguish civilian targets from military ones, reasoning that ordinary taxpayers were guilty of financing U.S. aggressions.

From 1998 to 2004, Al Qaeda shook western hearts through sensational suicide bombings and raids. The U.S. government and media dramatised the incidents, promoting the nomadic bin Laden as an evil genius who deserved annihilation. Some cynics went to the extent of claiming that he was an over–hyped 'Western creation'. Among extremist Muslims, his gall to stand up to the superpower assured cult status. With the September 11 strikes, he achieved what no other force on earth had done since 1812, attacking mainland America with devastating impact.

So manic was bin Laden's assault that the U.S. launched two wars in his name in 2001 (Afghanistan) and 2003 (Iraq). A $25 million reward notwithstanding, he evaded the American dragnet and released chilling tape-recorded messages to the media, urging fresh uprisings against the U.S. and its allies. As of 2005, the world's most wanted fugitive continues to remain on the most wanted list.

Yasser Arafat

1929 – 2004

The Palestinian cause

Yasser Arafat, the revolutionary Palestine Liberation Organisation (PLO) leader, was born in a wealthy family. His father was a successful trader. Arafat himself claimed that he was born in Jerusalem, although his birth certificate stated that he was born in Cairo. Christened Mohammed, Arafat was nicknamed Yasser. When his mother died five years after Arafat was born, a married uncle took care of him at his father's request.

Arafat became quite active in Muslim Brotherhood (Ikhwan) politics and was drawn in with a group that acted as liaison for German submarines that dropped arms for the Palestinians in Gaza. Soon, his revolutionary instincts got the better of him, and they came to the fore when he helped organise several Arab guerrilla groups in the 1950s. This included Al Fatah, a part of the PLO. In the early 1960s, Arafat was instrumental in planning a host of Al Fatah-led raids against Israel. Israel responded by pounding PLO bases in Lebanon.

Arafat studied at the University of Cairo and earned a degree in civil engineering. He founded the Palestinian Students' Union and also became its President. When his brother Badir was killed in an Israeli raid, Arafat volunteered for the Egyptian army, and was trained by the Egyptian Intelligence Service. In 1955, he re-joined the University as a Lieutenant. He later founded the General Union of Palestinian Students (GUPS), under the 'Aegis' of Egyptian intelligence. He popularised Nasserism and loyalty to Egypt. When a rival challenged GUPS' allegiance to Egypt, Arafat had him exterminated. Arafat's first appearance on the international stage came when he led a GUPS delegation at an international students' convention in Prague.

When Arafat addressed the United Nations General Assembly (1974), he established himself on the world political stage. The UN recognised the PLO as the representative of the Arabs of Palestine. Sporting a scarcely disguised pistol and carrying an olive branch, and dressed in a military uniform, Arafat's dramatic appearance stirred world awareness for the Palestinian cause. In the same year, the Palestine National Council adopted a policy of gradual liberation of Palestine. It declared the setting up of a Palestinian State.

In his formative years, Arafat was greatly inspired by his teacher, Majid Halaby, who actually gave him his nickname Yasser, because of his similarity to Yasser al Birah, a Palestinian leader, who was killed by the British. When Halaby was eventually killed in a factional variance,

▶ The Palestinian cause

Arafat formed a society for the martyr in his school. Historians also register the fact that Arafat fought against the Jews in 1948. It is also said that Arafat had a liking for drama. He is believed to have once shot himself in the leg to attract publicity as much as diversion.

Arafat vehemently claimed to have been in Jerusalem when the State of Israel was declared (1948). However, some historians believe that he may have returned to Gaza and planned a raid on Nizzanim. It was also from Gaza that Arafat took part in several terrorist activities. His vendetta was not just aimed against Jews, but also supporters of the Nashashibi band, his antagonists.

Arafat was elected Chairman of the Executive Committee of the PLO in 1969. He replaced Ahmed Shuqhairy, when his Al Fateh faction took control of the PLO. He quickly responded to Egypt's losing its face in the disastrous 6-day war with a master move. He alienated the PLO from pan-Arabist ideals to emphasis on total liberation of the Palestinian people.

When Arafat was appointed Commander-in-Chief of the All-Palestinian, Arab Guerilla Forces in 1970, the PLO was forced out of Jordan. This was a direct result of the Palestinian groups' attempted plans to dislodge the government of King Hussein. Arafat's PLO now wriggled itself out of the impasse and made its entry into Beirut. The Lebanese capital became headquarters for PLO operations against Israel till the early 1980s.

In a smart move under Arafat's leadership, the PLO, quietly 'Detached' itself from terrorist attacks against Israeli civilians and airplane hijackings. It is a matter of record that Arafat offered himself to mediate the release of hostages in the infamous Entebbe hijacking in Uganda in 1976. But, the role of Arafat in clandestine operations, including the brutal massacre of Israeli athletes in the Olympic Games in Munich (1972) and the Black September (1973) attack on the Saudi Embassy in Khartoum, Sudan, has long been alleged, if not proven.

In November 1988, Arafat proclaimed the independent Palestinian State – it was a symbolic announcement, because the PLO did not have control of any Palestinian territory. It was Arafat and PLO's clever move to promote home-grown revolt, the Intifadah, against Israel, which aroused passions in the West Bank and the Gaza Strip. However, Palestinian moderates and other temperate leaders across the world impressed upon Arafat to respond to American pressure and also accept UN Resolution 242 that recognises the existence of Israel.

In 1989, Arafat was elected by the Central Council of the PLO as the first President of the State of Palestine. The PLO was now supported by Saddam Hussein, which prompted Arafat to support the Iraqi invasion of Kuwait and oppose Allied operations against Iraq. In 1992 Arafat and the PLO held secret talks with Israel. This led to the signing of the Oslo Peace Accord between the PLO and Israel, which also established the platform for Palestinian-ruled territory in 1994. Arafat, Yitzhak Rabin, and Shimon Peres, shared the Nobel Peace Prize in 1994, for their key roles in the peace process.

For a man who is widely believed to have amassed enormous personal wealth from finances meant for the PLO, Arafat married a Christian Palestinian, Suha Taweel, in 1990. Suha gave birth to a daughter, Zahwa. Separated from Arafat, prior to his death in 2004, Suha continues to receive generous financial assistance from the Palestinian movement.

World leaders gathered in Egypt for Yasser Arafat's funeral on Friday November 12th 2004. The Palestinian leader died of a lengthy and unknown illness at a Paris hospital. Arafat was buried at the West Bank city of Ramallah. Arafat, had hoped to be buried in Jerusalem but was denied that by Israel. As word spread of Arafat's death, Palestinians gathered in the streets in the West Bank and Gaza and at his former headquarters in Ramallah.

Muammar Qaddafi

1942 –

Dictator and strongman

Muammar Qaddafi, Libyan leader and strongman, was the youngest child from a nomadic Bedouin peasant family. Qaddafi graduated from the University of Libya, with BA, in 1963. He became an army officer in 1965. Five years later, he formed, along with a group of fellow officers, a secret revolutionary committee and led a successful bloodless coup against the monarchy of King Idris I. Qaddafi quickly established himself as Libya's Commander–in–Chief and Chairman of the Revolutionary Command Council.

He brought into prominence a synthesis of Arab nationalism, revolutionary socialism, and Islamic orthodoxy. This provided him the base to run Libya's government on orthodox lines with a fierce hatred for the West. A year after Qaddafi seized power, he ordered the closure of the British and American military bases. This was followed by a government decree that confiscated the property of Libya's Italian and Jewish communities and nationalisation of foreign petroleum assets.

A votary of ancient Quranic law of cutting off the hands of thieves, Qaddafi also went onto to ban gambling and alcoholic beverages. Besides, he wanted to unify Libya with other Arab countries, including two of the region's leading nations, Egypt and Tunisia. In the process, he did not relax his bitter opposition of Israel. It is a matter of record that Qaddafi's government has been known for its support of many international terrorist and guerrilla organisations, including the Irish Republican Army (IRA), the Palestine Liberation Organisation (PLO), besides a host of extremist Arab and Islamic groups. This led to the U.S. bombing of Libya's alleged terrorist activities in 1986. A survivor,

Qaddafi managed to hold his country by the skin of his teeth, in the wake of the pounding, although this resulted in injury and death to several of his children.

A dictator known for his fundamentalism just as much as his impeccable attire, Qaddafi's first move as Libyan leader focused on altering the Libyan calendar. He published the 'Green Book', a series of three of booklets on democracy, economics, and sociology. Quite ironical, because he had played host to Carlos, the Jackal, the infamous assassin. It is also strongly believed that Qaddafi ordered the bombing of Pan Am Flight 103, which blew up in December 1988, over Lockerbie, Scotland. It was only in 2003 that Libya agreed to recompense $2.7 billion to families of the 270 killed on board the airplane.

It is said that Qaddafi may have pumped in finance for the 'Black September Movement,' which carried out the brutal massacre of Israeli players during the 1972 Munich Olympics. An avid sports fan, Qaddafi acquired a 7.5 per cent share of the famed Italian football club Juventus for US$21 million in 2002. He also had a long partnership with the late Gianni Agnelli, the primary investor in Fiat. In July 2004, Qaddafi became involved with chess: FIDE, the game's world governing body, provided Prize Money for the World Championship held in Tripoli.

A mercurial persona, Qaddafi never sleeps in the same place for two days in a row. He trusts no one, and is always said to have a personal guard detail who under oath are expected to die on his behalf in any eventuality.

The only certainty despite his monumental follies, is his almost–impregnable control of his country, the army, and its political machinery.

DICTATORS & TYRANTS

Idi Amin

1923/1928 – 2003

Military dictator of Uganda

General Idi Amin Dada Oumee, the (in)famous military dictator of Uganda (1971-1979), was born in the Kakwa tribe, in the West Nile Arua District. The exact year of his birth is not known, because there is no existing birth record against his name. Historians suggest 1923 to 1928 as being the probable years of his birth but this makes no difference to his legacy, or his sinister crimes against humanity. What is on record is the fact that Amin used to celebrate his birthday on January 1.

Brought up by his mother, a witch doctor, Amin was not formally educated. A man with a grave outlook, Amin took tribalism, Uganda's most nagging problem, to its horrific depths. He not only ordered the hounding of Acholi, Lango, and other tribes, but tortured and killed between 100,000 and 300,000 Ugandans during his rule as President.

Amin first enrolled in the King's African Rifles of the British–ruled colony as a Private in 1946. He quietly climbed to the rank of Lieutenant following action during the Mau Mau revolt in Kenya. His officers thought of him to be a skilled, ambitious soldier, with a proclivity for brutality. He marched ahead in his army career and became a Sergeant–Major, following which he was bestowed with the position of an Effendi which was the highest rank for a Black African in the British Army. Amin dabbled in sports. He was considered to be a brilliant swimmer. He also held Uganda's light–heavyweight boxing championship for ten years (1951–1960). There seemed to be no opposition to the pugilist in one of the world's most sadistic leaders–to–be, in the country.

Uganda achieved independence from British rule in 1962. When Milton Obote became the free nation's first Prime Minister, Amin was made Captain. Two years later, he was promoted as Deputy Commander of the Ugandan army. It was not long before Obote and his loyalist Amin were mired in a deal to smuggle gold, coffee, and ivory, from the Democratic Republic of the Congo. A parliamentary investigation put Obote on the edge. He quickly promoted his henchman Amin to General and made him Chief–of–Staff. Obote now swooped on five ministers and annulled the Ugandan constitution. He also declared himself as the new President. 'King' Freddie, the ousted President, who had fled Uganda, died in exile in Britain.

When Amin began enlisting members of his own tribe into the army, Obote was totally opposed. This led to hostility between the old friends. Obote made his first move to place his Chief–of–Staff under house arrest.

► Military dictator of Uganda

Previous page: Amin gave Uganda's 60–70,000 Asian inhabitants three months to leave the country (1972). He said this was what God had told him to do in his dreams. Opposite: Witnesses have recorded that Amin decapitated Obote's supporters and ordered their heads to be laid on his dining table.

His idea failed. He now gave Amin a non–executive position in the army. When Obote was attending a Commonwealth summit in Singapore (1971), Amin with covert support of Rwandan exiles, who had no love lost for Obote, staged a coup d'etat. Amin declared himself the new President – and, Obote went into self–exile.

Amin nattily gave 'King' Freddie a state burial. He unchained many political prisoners, and fragmented the Secret Police. He also promised to hold elections. It was a calculated move to win popular support both within the country and abroad. Amin was welcomed, though some mediapersons, who had met him in all his magnificence, thought of him as a weird and bizarre character.

For a man who loved racing cars, boxing, and Disney cartoons, Amin was also considered a jovial man. He could at times sound childish. This was not given the thought it deserved, because behind the veneer of his pranks Amin was ruthlessly callow within. This was noticed by the British army officers under whom he had served earlier. Not by the world.

Amin, who is said to have sired tens of children, began to now make his moves to liquidate Obote's supporters. This also included the intelligentsia, for whom he had no place in his scheme of things. Witnesses have recorded that Amin even decapitated them and ordered their heads to be laid on his dining table. He is said to have heaped vitriol on them for not proclaiming support for him, while nibbling at their flesh.

Obote tried to ignite a coup against Amin, from Tanzania. He failed in his attempt. Enraged, Amin bombed Tanzanian towns, and flushed out Acholi and Lango officers, who were Obote's sympathisers. Amin's vicious act led to ethnic violence and tens of thousands of abductions, tortures, rapes and murder by his troops. It is also reported that Amin himself ordered the execution of Janani Luwum, the Anglican Archbishop of Uganda,

Benedicto Kiwanuka, the Chief Justice, Frank Kalimuzo, the Chancellor of Makerere University, Joseph Mubiru, the Governor of the Bank of Uganda, and many ministers. Amin was paranoid about their true intentions and suspected them to have fomented revolt against his presidentship.

Amin also gave Uganda's 60–70,000 Asian inhabitants three months to leave the country (1972). He said this was what God had told him to do in his dreams. Asians were Ugandan citizens; they owned numerous businesses in the country. Amin now used the money from their businesses to recompense soldiers devoted to him. He also cut off diplomatic relations with Israel and Britain. He now sought Muammar Qaddafi of Libya and the Soviet Union for support and aid.

Amin had close relations with the Palestine Liberation Organisation (PLO). He offered the Israeli embassy to them as headquarters. When Flight 139, the Air France A–300B Airbus, was hijacked from Athens, in June 1976, Amin welcomed the hijackers to land at Entebbe International Airport in Uganda's capital, Kampala. The hijackers wanted the release of 53 PLO prisoners in exchange for 256 hostages. They were backed by Amin's own troops. Amin visited the hostages in all his grandeur, and asked them to sing praises for him. But, Israel had other plans.

When Israeli paratroopers stormed the airport and freed the hostages, Amin felt like a caged tiger. Uganda's Air Force was a mute spectator to the spectacular rescue operation. It was in a shambles, thanks to Israel's meticulously–planned assault.

This was the beginning of Amin's downfall. Idi Amin died in a Saudi Arabian hospital on August 16, 2003 of multiple organ failure. Human rights groups and Ugandan government officials expressed their disappointment that Amin never faced trial for his crimes.

Al Capone

1899 – 1947

Synonymous with crime

Born in New York to poor Italian immigrants Al Capone grew up in a neighbourhood awash with criminal activity. After Capone quit school at age 14, he took on odd jobs, and became a member of a notorious gang in Manhattan. It was while working as a bartender that Capone received his facial scars. This led to his nickname, 'Scarface.'

When he was just 20, Capone went to Chicago to work for a fraudster. He had a born knack for the bizarre and with a plethora of gangland shootings in his resume, the sharp Capone was very soon in control of the city's large–scale criminal activity. Capone's gang held control of liquor, gambling, flesh trade and sex rackets.

Capone built a niche for himself by giving huge pay–offs to corrupt police officers and politicians. In the course of time, Capone's empire extended to become a standard for modern organised–crime. However, despite his open criminal operations, Capone became a celebrity. He was a regular visitor at theatres and sports grounds and was also often seen entertaining his VIP guests with his extraordinary opulence.

Capone's favourite gunmen were alleged to have indulged in many dastardly crimes, including the murder of seven members of a rival gang in what is famously referred to as the St. Valentine's Day Massacre (1929). The charge was never proved.

First indicted for his rowdy conduct while he was working for Frankie Yale, Capone's criminal intensity flashed itself quite early in his lawless career. He had murdered two men while in New York. But, what made him more ruthless was the gangland protocol, where no one admitted to hearing or seeing a thing. Capone got away with his evil acts and returned to Chicago when the dust had settled, and quickly moved his family into a house.

It was Yale's old mentor, John Torrio, who first noticed a rare flash in Capone – a deadly combination of physical strength and intelligence. Torrio groomed Capone, and it did not take long for the protègè to assist Torrio manage his bootlegging business. Capone became Torrio's most trusted aide, and a full partner in his saloons, gambling houses, and brothels.

Capone became the boss when Torrio was shot by rival gang members and decided to leave Chicago for good. He now began to call the shots and not without reason. His men liked, trusted, and followed him. Capone began his expansion plans and also his syndication of the city's vice industry. He now controlled speakeasies, bookie joints, gambling houses, brothels, horse and race tracks, nightclubs, distilleries and breweries. Between 1925 and 1930, Capone's income was estimated at $100,000,000 a year. A wily operator, Capone further extended his grip by pumping his monies into the largest cleaning and dyeing plant chain in his crime capital of Chicago.

Capone killed dozens of people with his own hands. Paradoxically, he treated people fairly and generously. He was a criminal with a respect for honour so long as the equation suited him. Notwithstanding his dark side, Capone also played the Good Samaritan during the Great Depression. He was the first to open soup kitchens. He also forced traders to provide clothes and food to the needy at his expense.

In the end, a federal jury convicted Capone of income–tax evasion. He spent over seven years in prison, and, thereafter, retired to his mansion in Florida, where he died (1947) from complications due to syphilis. Capone's dubious achievements far outlived his myth – a man who made Chicago synonymous with crime.

Adolf Hitler

1889 - 1945

Irascible tyrant

Adolf Hitler was born in a tiny township near Linz (Upper Austria), which was then Austria–Hungary, close to the border with Germany. His father was a small–time customs executive.

Some historians speculate that Hitler was part–Jewish, though evidence for it is wanting. However, it is a recorded fact that Hitler was quite clever although he had failed a couple of times in high school admission tests in Linz. But, failure gave him a dividend. He became a big fan of Professor Leopold Poetsch, who significantly predisposed the young man's outlook on Pan–German identity.

Hitler hoped to become an artist, at age eighteen. He had an orphan's allowance. He worked as a freelance illustrator and drew homes and palatial buildings. His application to the Vienna school of art was rejected twice. To add salt to his wounds, he lost his annuity in 1910. He had inherited some money from his aunt and as soon as he was finished with it, he began to sell his painted postcards for a living. He hardly made enough money for himself, but managed to attend operas and read books.

It was at this time that the flagrant bulb of anti–Semitism was lit in his mind. He also began to ingrain anti–Jewish ideas from politicians, and evolve on his theory of the 'Aryan race,' and its superior nature which became the foundation of his political thought. He was also now convinced that the Jews were the natural enemies of the Aryans; they were instrumental for Germany's economic troubles.

Found unfit in his first attempt, Hitler saw army service during World War I. He was not an extraordinary soldier, but was bestowed with awards for bravery. It was during this time that he had his first taste of poison gas from which he miraculously escaped. When Germany surrendered, he was aghast. He was infuriated with civilian politicians for betraying German ascendancy.

Soon enough, Hitler latched on to the spectre of the scapegoat theory of 'International Jewry' that led to World War I and Germany's ignominious defeat. In July 1919, he became, thanks to his skilled rhetoric, an 'Inspirational Speaker.' He influenced soldiers and others and now nursed the idea of forming his own party, although he worked for the Nationalist Party. Once he became its leader, he changed its name to National Socialist German Workers Party, or the (in)famous Nazi Party .

▶ Irascible tyrant

Previous page: Eva Braun first met Hitler while working as a photographers assistant. The attraction was immediate but Hitler avoided any suggestion of intimacy.
Opposite: A soldier inspects the room where Braun and Hitler bit into vials of cyanide – Hitler shot himself at the same time.

Hitler quickly began to demonstrate his two amazing talents of public speaking and arousing personal loyalty in whosoever listened to his magnetic oratorical skills. He attracted many followers, and soon got into the act of ousting Bavaria's right–wing separatist government, and taking over control of Berlin. His grand formula failed and he was arrested.

He landed in prison but it gave him the time to dictate his book, 'Mein Kampf,' or the story of his struggle, to his deputy Rudolf Hess. He was thought harmless and released. Soon, Hitler established a personal bodyguard, the Schutzstaffel (the dreaded SS). It was commanded by Heinrich Himmler, who later became the principal architect of Hitler's diabolical plans to exterminate Jews during World War II.

Hitler now began to cleverly use the firm pitch of insulted national pride that was the result of the Treaty of Versailles, which had stifled the defeated German Empire. Germany not only lost territory in Europe and its colonies, the Treaty forced it to admit accountability for the war, and offer recompense ($6,600,000). This was the magic wand he wanted – and, he lost no time using it with stunning effect.

Depression was also another great opportunity. Hitler won the admiration of German farmers, war veterans, the middle–class, and the unemployed. While the urban community scoffed at him, Hitler turned the tables.

Hitler was officially sworn in as Chancellor in the Reichstag (January 1933). He made one decree after the other, and solicited the army to affirm a pledge of loyalty to him, personally – an unparalleled move.

Hitler projected himself as Germany's saviour. He said it was providence that placed in his hands the proviso to overcome Depression, the communists, the Versailles Treaty and, of course, the Jews. He lost no time and engineered the greatest expansion of German industrial production. Civil improvement reached its peak and his government generated near full employment. He also scored another major victory with his health policies aimed at children and mothers. Architecture also became a subject of German pride.

In 1935 Hitler rejected the Treaty of Versailles and armed Germany with a modern army and air force. The following year, he took control of the demilitarised zone in the Rhineland. Britain and France stayed silent. He was emboldened. He tested his air force during the Spanish Civil War, and was proud of its might. He quickly formed an alliance with the Italian dictator Benito Mussolini and expanded the arrangement with Japan, Hungary, Romania and Bulgaria.

During the years 1942–1945, the SS methodically massacred over 3.5 million Jews in concentration camps. This was called the Holocaust, a catastrophe totally beyond comprehension. Hitler also exterminated hundreds of thousands of others, including mentally deficient people, not to speak of millions of others during the war from Poland to the Soviet Union.

He also became 'Time' magazine's Man of the Year (1938). But, when he entered Czechoslovakia, Britain and France declared war on Germany. Hitler marched on to France and he soon conquered the Netherlands and Belgium. Britain was now on its knees. Buoyed by his magnificent triumphs, Hitler envisioned the conquest of Russia, with which he had earlier made a covert pact. It was a huge misadventure and blunder. Germany was defeated at the Battle of Stalingrad and the tide had now turned. When the U.S. entered the war in December 1941, Hitler, a megalomaniac, was now caged from all sides.

When the Russians closed in on Berlin, Hitler, confined to his own bunker, shot himself with a pistol.

A dark chapter in history was finally over.